The Blessings
Of Forgiveness

The Blessings Of Forgiveness

THE HEALING JOURNEY OF
BLAISE LABBE

CEDRIC D. FISHER & COMPANY
PUBLISHERS

Editor: Lola M. Fisher
Cover Designer: Sandra Schwartzman
Editorial Designer: Norma L. Ortiz / Sandra Schwartzman

Library of Congress - 2024912886
ISBN eBook- 979-8-9911634-9-1
ISBN Hardback- 979-8-9911634-2-2
ISBN Paperback: 979-8-9922459-2-9

Contents

Foreword

by Paula Madison

It begins with Colorism. Colorism - a subset of racism, shaped Blaise Labbe's early life long before he emerged from his brown-skinned mother's womb. He was born into a Louisiana social structure that robbed him of a teen father. His father was forced to deny him because of colorism within his own family. Blaise was reared by a circle of women and men whose own struggles with racism and poverty were dominated by colorism.

His story begins centuries before Ignatius Blaise Labbe was born in the 1960s South. In the 1600s, French colonizers introduced a heinous form of oppression to the West Africans, who were enslaved and subsequently brutalized on the plantations of Louisiana.

The combination of the vestiges of slavery plus the religion imposed upon them by the Roman Catholic Church resulted in a color-caste system so heinous that its vestiges destroyed any hope that a young high school couple who conceived a son could live together in love. And this begins the story of Blaise Labbe. The young lovers' hopes of a life together were shattered because he was fair-skinned, and she was not. This colorism drove a never-ending wedge between African Americans based on the amount of melanin in the skin.

Two "color-struck daughters of the church" — Catholic nuns and the young man's aunts — deemed his sepia-colored love interest too dark to be accepted into their "light, bright, almost white" family. And it was this world into which their young son Blaise was born to his unwed teen mother.

Two families' misbegotten plot to keep the young lovers apart led to suicide, conspiracies, lies, abuse, and secrets that haunted Blaise for much of his early life and which led him to attempt suicide as his despondent father had before him.

Throughout his early life, Blaise was never aware that the man who occasionally showed up to show him kindness was, in fact, his father. And when a stepfather appeared in his life, Blaise was still a young boy. This stepfather offered no love or care for the determined and resilient child who would later grow up to be inducted into the Oklahoma Journalism Hall of Fame.

During childhood, he experienced kindness and cruelty from neighbors and strangers while he sought his place in their small town. At times, the identities of his cousins, teachers, playmates, parents, grandparents, half-brother, half-sisters, aunties, uncles, and shopkeepers morphed and changed. If Blaise's true north was his mother, she was ill-equipped to guide him. Because of colorism, she had flunked the brown paper bag test—innocently failing her son.

This book tells of racism, emotional abuse, manipulation, and sorrow, but it's so much more than that. It is the story of a child who refused to succumb to interracial discrimination, fought depression and deception, and through it all, became an exceptional man who found the strength within to overcome the destiny that his dysfunctional, ill-fated family set forth for him.

Journalist, husband, father, community leader, and person of great faith, Ignatius Blaise Labbe is my brother-friend. He overcame the odds to become A Good Man. Here is his story.

Acknowledgments

I want to thank my family, who, through everything that has transpired over the years, have put our Heavenly Father first and understood the importance of what family truly means. I especially want to thank my wife and kids, who supported me and encouraged me to tell my story. I have been blessed with many wonderful people; thank you for sharing my journey. Most importantly, I want to thank Yahweh, our Heavenly Father, for helping me understand that "to those that love Yahweh, all things work together for good, even to them that are called according to his purpose."

My Early Years

This is my story—the story of Ignatius Blaise Labbe. It's a story about forgiveness and healing, discovering who I am, and the joy and pain during the journey. It's a story about a family's journey from brokenness to blessing.

I was born in Lafayette, Louisiana, and grew up on North Washington Street. I was the oldest of four siblings. I lived in Lafayette from birth to five years old. My mom didn't know what she wanted to name me when I was born. One day, she talked to a nun before I was born, and the nun told her she should name me Ignatius Blaise after Saint Ignatius de Loyola and Saint Blaise of Sebaste, who is honored by the blessing of the throat. I go by my middle name, Blaise. Everyone has always called me Blaise since I was a child, so that became the name I used and associated most with instead of my first name, Ignatius. My mom gave me a nickname when I was a kid. She called me Iggy, which was short for Ignatius.

I have one sister who is two years younger, another sister who is four years younger, and a brother who is seven years younger than me.

My earliest memories are great and began when I was only three. Looking back over my life, I think about how we didn't have much. But I would have never known that as a kid. I know that's cliché-ish, but it's the truth.

I grew up in a three-room house with my mom. We had a living room, another room in the middle of the house—the bedroom, and a kitchen. If I count the little bathroom in the back, we had four rooms. That was our house. It doesn't sound like much to brag about, but to a little kid, it was a castle.

As a kid, I wasn't afraid of much. In Louisiana, especially in Southwest Louisiana, a fear was instilled in children. People would talk about voodoo and would tell you to go to bed early or the boogeyman or whatever would get you. They would tell the kids, "You should cover your toes with the blanket because the boogeyman will start pulling them at night if they are sticking out."

As a younger kid, crazy stuff like that played in my mind. I was terrified just thinking about a boogeyman pulling on my toes at night, but I didn't fear much as I got older.

I had no concept of a dad when I was a child, and I didn't realize I didn't have one. I had my mom, great-aunt, great-great aunt, and uncle (my mom's brother). That was my family. I was okay with that, and I was happy. My world centered around my immediate family. That was my world, and nothing seemed out of place. When I was five years old, this man came into our lives. Suddenly, I had a dad, but I will give more details later about how he came into our lives.

We lived on a quarter-mile strip in the 100 block of North Washington Street. My great-aunt, Anna Mae Deverges, and great-great-aunt, Mary Martinez, who raised my mom, uncle, and me, lived right next door. On that quarter-mile strip, we had relatives who lived across the street. Another great-aunt, Hazel Deverges, her daughters who were like my aunts, and her mother, Mrs. Moda, another great-great-aunt, lived next door to her.

Another lady, Miss Bernice, was their neighbor. Miss Bernice was related to us, but I don't know how. A dead-end street was connected to our quarter-mile strip on Washington Street. It was called Patton Street, and we had more relatives who lived on that dead-end street. In the 1960s, the Black part of town was divided into seven sections. The section of Lafayette where I grew up was called Fightingville. Even though the little section of Washington Street where I grew up was peaceful, that part of town was rough. The entire section consisted of about a 20-block area. Fightingville was an economically poor, Black neighborhood.

Everyone in the neighborhood was Black except one Cajun (White) family who lived in the last house on the corner of our part of Washington Street. It was a typical Black area where folks were proud of who they were. Everyone looked out for each other and respected their elders. It was a village where other people's parents could whip you if you were out of line, and they would not get in trouble. Imagine that happening today. I don't think so! As a kid, you knew where it was safe to go and where it was not. The grown-ups always told us to hang with someone we knew when we went to the grocery store or played outside. We didn't have to fear getting snatched up; the thing we feared was more about getting caught in some other issues that might have been going on, like the many fights that occurred in that area.

Fightingville was a dangerous part of town. Like

most low-income areas, crime was high. There were shootings and stabbings regularly in the neighborhood. We called a little section about three blocks from my house "*The Block*" because nightclubs were on each corner. From Wednesday through Sunday, at least one to two people would get killed on "*The Block*." Fightingville was not a safe area where kids could hang out. Back then, there weren't a lot of drugs or anything, but people fought all the time. You could be walking to a store, and there were gangsters in or around the store. There were certain people in the neighborhood that everyone knew were bad. Unless you were looking for trouble, you didn't go on "*The Block*," especially on Friday and Saturday nights. Drugs, prostitution, and gambling were prevalent in this area, and consequently, people lost their lives because of these dangerous situations.

One of the other things that was unique about Fightingville was how everyone had a hustle. Two ladies lived there, known as the Cold Cup ladies. They would make different flavored Kool-Aid and freeze them, then sell them for a nickel. Ladies would make lunches and sell them to working people in the neighborhood for lunch. The neighborhood folks called them "Plate Lunch" ladies. Some people in the neighborhood were known for poker nights because they hosted poker games, and there was always a place to shoot dice. My step-grandparents Alton and Mary Chaisson had some of the biggest weekend poker games in Fightingville. We are talking about thousands of dollars flowing through that house on Friday nights. On Saturdays, less money flowed though, but not by much. I guess people had to save a bit for Sunday's collection plate.

For most people, the hustling was about getting by and paying the bills. I'm sure folks wanted to leave Fightingville, and they probably worked very hard to get out, but many did not realize their dream of going beyond Fightingville. Back then and even to this day, it is one of those repetitive cycles of life. Most people still living in Fightingville are stuck there for the rest of their lives.

Most of the homes in Fightingville were three-room shotgun houses like the one I grew up in. Shotgun houses were narrow rectangular houses, usually no more than about 12 feet wide, with rooms arranged one behind the other and doors at each end of the house. They were a popular style of house built in the South from the end of the Civil War through the 1920s. There are different theories about the origin of the name "shotgun house." One theory is that the name may have come from how the houses were structured, meaning that a bullet shot from the front doors would pass through the house without hitting anything and exit through the back door.[1]

The shotgun houses in Fightingville had no central air conditioning. You were considered rich if you had a window air conditioning unit. Those without air conditioning would put electric fans in the window. We had little gas-lit heaters to heat the homes. The first time I saw a real lawnmower with a motor was around 1971. We used push mowers, the kind with the blades on them. I was born in 1965, so it was during that time that Fightingville residents used the push mowers. The houses were sitting on top of cinder blocks in case of flooding. There may have been a few brick homes, but there were only about four in my area. Almost every house had a swing on the front porch. On Sundays, the porch was the gathering place after church. Everyone, friends and family, sat on the front porch and talked.

We had chickens in little chicken coops in the backyard. When I was a little boy, my job was to run outside, grab a chicken, and watch my great aunt ring its neck.

1 Wikipedia, Shotgun House, version date - 3 December 2024, URL: https://en.wikipedia.org/wiki/Shotgun_house

She would boil the chicken and then remove the feathers. We also had little gardens in the backyard with peppers, tomatoes, green onions, and okra.

I had a cousin who was two years older than me. His full name was Aquinas Carlos Michael Domingue. Growing up, we ran around in diapers together. He was a big kid, not fat, just very muscular, even as a young child. He was very athletic in high school. He was an outstanding basketball player, as well as a baseball player. He was extremely close to his mom and grandmother, my great-aunt, Hazel Deverges. As kids, we were thick as thieves. We were so close that we hardly ever left one another's side. We played together every day, and when I moved away and would come back to visit, I stayed at his house. Our moms were close. He was more like a big brother than a cousin. His mom and my mom were first cousins.

We did many things together when we were growing up. Farmers used to grow sugarcane in a field behind my great aunt Hazel's house. Aquinas could break the sugarcane stocks because he was bigger and stronger than me. He and I would peel them back and chew on the stocks. They eventually noticed that some of the sugar canes kept coming up missing. When they discovered it was us, "Oh my gosh!" did we ever get in trouble! I will never forget getting our butts whipped for stealing those sugarcane stocks. We were always chasing the chickens that we had in the backyard. We would chase and mistreat them in some shape or form. We threw rocks or tried to hang them somehow, so we got in trouble. We didn't understand that those same chickens were our food.

We also got in trouble for horsing around on the railroad tracks. We lived alongside railroad tracks and would race the train or throw money on the tracks. We would wait for the crossings to go down, count the whistles from the train, and try to beat it at the crossing. We had some close calls with the train. But we had a much worse time when Grandma found out about it. Grandma would whip our butts for racing the train. The other fun game we played on the train tracks was taking nickels and placing them on the tracks. When the train came, the train would smash the nickels, sometimes almost the size of quarters. We would use those smashed nickels as quarters at the grocery stores to buy extra candy.

Later in life, as a college freshman, I'd become a pretty good pool player. That became my little side hustle.

My uncle Tony owned a nightclub called the Cockatoo. On Sundays, the Cockatoo was the place to be if you wanted to have a good time. It was in between Lafayette and Opelousas, Louisiana. Opelousas is known to have gorgeous young ladies. One night, my cousin Aquinas and I were talking to some young ladies, and these guys in the club from Opelousas were upset because the young ladies were also from Opelousas. They felt that we Lafayette boys shouldn't have been talking to their women. I challenged one of the guys to a pool game instead of fighting. He wanted to know what the stakes were. I told him that if I won, my cousin and I would go out with their ladies, and if they won, they could go out with my sister, Shelly, and my cousin, Stasia. To this day, Shelly and I laugh about that bet because Shelly was so mad that night that she threatened to kick my ass if I lost the game. Of course, I didn't lose, so everything ended well.

Unfortunately, Aquinas got caught up in that repetitive cycle in Fightingville. He worked very hard his whole life, but he had little to show for the work that he had done. Our priorities shifted and changed, and we just grew apart. Not only did our priorities change, but also our paths, so unfortunately, we lost touch and didn't communicate much anymore. It was probably more on my end than it was on his. Trust is a big thing to me, and once you break that trust, it's hard for me to allow you back into my life. I've been through a lot and have allowed people to take advantage of me. And as I've gotten older, the trust factor weighs heavily on me. We had a time when that trust was broken, and for me, it was hard to rebuild it. Sadly, he passed away in October 2024 before we had a chance to put the past behind us, reconnect, and restore our relationship.

One of the fascinating things about where we lived was this juke joint on the corner of Washington Street and the dead-end Patton Street. Some of the greatest Zydeco players in history, like Clifton Chenier and Rocky Dopsie, would come to the juke joint and play their music. Zydeco is a style of music that originated in Louisiana in the 20th century. It combines a variety of musical styles, including blues, rhythm and blues, Louisiana French accordion music, Afro-Caribbean beats, Creole, Cajun, Gospel, and Native American musical cultures.

The word "zydeco" comes from a Creole French expression "*les haricots sont pas sales*," which means "the snap beans ain't salty." This expression is a figure of speech, meaning "times are tough." Zydeco's origins predate the United States as a country. Still, it evolved into its present form in the 1950s under the influence of Clifton Chenier, who played his music at the Juke Joint and is often called the king of zydeco.[2]

On Sunday nights, the juke joint was the place to be if you wanted to listen to good Zydeco music and have a good time. Only a few houses were on the dead-end street not far from the Juke Joint.

Most Saturdays when I was a kid, I went to Hermann Park in Lafayette with my mom and her friends. It was a rite of passage for the neighborhood families with kids to go to Hyman Park. We would run around the park and have a blast. It was very cathartic because going to the park was one of my favorite activities. It was a place where I could run and play with my friends and my cousins. My mom, her friends, and everybody enjoyed talking and eating barbecue in the park. It was a ritual to go to Hyman Park, but we had to be back home by two o'clock. That was because Paul Thibeaux, "The House Rocker," who was Lafayette's first Black disc jockey, had a show that started then. He played top 40 music and all the Rhythm and Blues hits of that time from two

2 MasterClass, ZydecoMusic Guide: The Origin and Sound of Zydeco, Written by MasterClass. https://www.masterclass.com/articles/zydeco-music-guide#3ta1seLIQtNx6BcQTUuRbM

to four o'clock. Then, from four to six, he would play Louisiana Zydeco music. The juke joint got going around six-thirty or seven o'clock every Saturday. They played until about midnight. So, from about seven to midnight, the juke joint was hopping.

Another thing of note about that area was the Miller distributorship on Patton Street. Because our family dominated that little quarter-mile strip, everybody knew us. The Miller Distributorship folks knew my great-great-aunt, Hazel Deverges, quite well. They would sometimes give her free beer. That was their way of promoting and drumming up business. People would sit on her porch and drink beer, especially on Sundays. Everyone knew and loved my great aunt Hazel because she was "nuts."

Aunt Hazel was the life of the party, even if there was no party. Her big personality and great wit made people gravitate to her. She was swift to respond with a comment if you challenged her. She would cut you, and you wouldn't even know it. She would have been great at playing the dozens. She loved to drink alcohol. Once, when a fire raged behind her home in an open field, the firefighters came and told her she needed to evacuate. She told them she couldn't leave because her children were in the house. The firefighters were confused about her having children because she was in her eighties. They looked around the house and found no one. They asked her to leave, and she repeated she couldn't go because of her kids, so the firefighters looked for pets and found nothing. So, they returned to her and asked her to clarify where her kids were. She told them under the bed, in the bathroom cabinets, and a drawer under the stove. The firefighters looked and found bottles of whiskey. She thanked the firemen for saving her "kids" and evacuated the house.

Sundays were the best days because we would go to church, and there was a bakery across the street from the church. We would stop at the bakery after church to get donuts and then go home. As Black folks in the South are known to do, we'd have a gigantic late lunch or early dinner, whichever way you look at it. After dinner, we kids would go outside to play. "Oh my gosh!" Then, man, at 6 o'clock, people would come from all over. This was Louisiana, so the weather was hot most of the year. We'd sit on the porch, and then old folks would be on their swings. It would be dark, but we'd sit out there until 9 or 10 p.m. just listening to the live music coming from the juke joint. It was so magical. I mean, it was a blessed life.

Years later, I was going to college in Lafayette, and guess where we were on Saturdays, in the park. All my cousins, friends, and I were in the same park, doing the same things as adults. It was a lot of fun doing those same things we did as kids: eating barbecue, hanging out, and having a good time. Nobody was doing anything crazy. We didn't do drugs or anything stupid. We just had good old-fashioned fun. It was very ironic for me. I had a cousin who loved the music group Zap. He had an old brown Camaro and would turn his music up so loud we could hear him before he entered the park. Everyone would yell, "Uptown in the House". His nickname was Uptown. He got the nickname because he played basketball and was not that good. He would shoot the ball from the "top of the key" or the corner when he got in a game. The "top of the key" is the area of the basketball court we now call three-point land. He would jack up shots, and they rarely went in. He would shoot so far out, hence the nickname Uptown. Uptown's real name is Keith Sonnier. Keith was one from Fightingville who broke the repetitive cycle. He became an assistant fire chief. Unfortunately, Keith passed away a few years ago. I was at a Mardi Gras ball in February 2022 and ran into Keith months before he passed away. I felt very fortunate that we at least got to see one another again before he passed away. I remember the good times we had together. We would hang out and have a blast.

My Passions

My uncle, my mom's brother, Tony Chassion, was my hero. He was the first male influence I had. He was a drum major in high school. That was a big deal because he attended an all-Black private catholic school, Holy Rosary Institute. The band was patterned after the world-famous Grambling State Marching Band. So, becoming the drum major was equivalent to being the football team's star quarterback. After high school, he went to Vietnam.

When he returned from Vietnam, he became very interested in the Black Power movement and civil rights at the height of the movement. He was very adamant because when veterans came back from Vietnam, people mistreated them, but not only that, Black veterans were especially mistreated. And in Louisiana, there was still a lot of racism and prejudice. So, he got actively involved in the civil rights movement. He pushed for rights for Blacks.

He participated in protests at drug store counters,

protested, marched, and did sit-ins. He was very vocal and would have stump speeches. He did many things to make our community a better place for Blacks. He used his GI bill to go to college. He was very vocal about civil rights, even in college.

When I was about four or five, probably four, the police came to our house. They were banging on the door, and then they burst through the door and arrested my uncle. I didn't understand what was happening because I was only a child. I screamed we have to help him! Someone said we would have to get him a lawyer. But we didn't have the money to hire a lawyer. He spent maybe two days in jail; then they let him out. The police eventually dropped all the charges against him. The charges against him were disturbing the peace or something like that. That experience didn't deter him; it only forced him to do more. He continued fighting for the rights of Blacks. The police never arrested him again.

Due to the influence of my uncle, being undeterred, standing for what I believe, and helping people became my passion, too. So, I figured my path was to become a lawyer. I wanted to be a lawyer because I saw what happened to my uncle. That was my goal until I was 20. If you were to ask anybody when I was a child, they would say, "he wants to be a lawyer." I wanted to be an advocate for people. I went to school and majored in criminal justice. I was determined that's what I wanted to do. Over the years, I read many stories about the unjust arrest of Blacks. I saw the justice system didn't favor Blacks regarding getting fairly treated. So, I wanted to be that person who would defend my people and others who otherwise would not get a fair shake. I wanted to be a defense attorney.

That was how strong an influence my uncle had on me. But I was not the only one he influenced. You see, he had one of those personalities everybody gravitated to. He was very quick on his feet. He had a hustler's mentality. Some people would say he had a great gift of gab, and others would say he was a great bullshit artist. It was amazing to watch him because he could be on the street with gangsters, and he'd fit right in. On the other side, he was good friends with politicians. One was Edwin Edwards, the former governor of Louisiana.

Many White people feared him because he had a bold personality and was well-spoken. In the late 60s and early 70s, White people in the South were not used to young people, especially young Black people, speaking up and speaking out about injustices, especially in

Louisiana. Blacks were supposed to accept their fate and stay in their place. My uncle Tony didn't believe he had a place, and he challenged them by stepping out of bounds that were long established. When he was going to college, he soaked up everything. He learned as much as he could about everything. He knew city government ordinances in and out. He knew state law in and out. And so, he challenged judges and city council representatives. Years after he was arrested, he learned the art of negotiation and made friends with the movers and shakers in Lafayette. He began to have influence and a voice in the political realm in the city. He was elected to the Lafayette School Board in 1971. He eventually owned his own business. My uncle helped employ a lot of Blacks within the school system.

The school district doesn't own buses, so they contract the service out. One contractor later became my brother-in-law. My brother-in-law got a bus and a contract with the school board with help from my uncle Tony. Uncle Tony had a lot of weight and influence in Lafayette. Deep down, he was very kind and soft-hearted. But when he needed to be, he was a skillful politician who was fierce in debates, conversations, or whatever the situation was. Uncle Tony could intimidate people, but people also just loved him.

One time, an elderly Black couple was leaving a mall parking lot, and their car hit a White gentleman's car; the White man just went off on the elderly couple. He started yelling, "I'm going to sue you for everything you have. I was with my uncle Tony, and we just happened to drive up on the incident. My uncle got out of his car, and everyone stopped. Someone said, "Oh, Mr. Chaisson, how are you doing?" The White gentleman said, "These people hit our car." Watching my uncle talk to both parties was impressive, and seeing the police let him do his thing was inspiring.

Uncle Tony talked to the Black couple because they were scared. He told them, "Don't worry, we'll take care of it. Then, out of nowhere, Tony asked the White gentleman, "How much damage do you think you have realistically?" The gentleman said about $1,000 or something around there. My uncle said, "Nope, I don't think so. You will not be suing them for that much money, but I'll make it worthwhile." I watched my uncle pull out a cash roll, peel off $500, and pay the guy for his damages. The Black couple was crying and vowed to pay my uncle back. Tony told them not to worry about it; everything was all good. That's the kind of person my uncle was. He was just a great guy.

Uncle Tony had a sad ending to his life. He passed away at the age of 47 or 48 from cancer. The unfortunate thing is, for all the good and the great things that he did, he eventually succumbed to drugs. He was a smoker and, unfortunately, got caught up with the wrong folks and started abusing drugs. I was living in Houston when my great-aunt Hazel called me and said I needed to come home. It's a three-hour drive from Houston to Lafayette. I asked my aunt, "What's going on?" She said, "You should come get your uncle because he's not doing well. He's in bad shape." We knew Uncle Tony was on drugs, but we didn't realize how bad it was. They wanted me to get him because after they found him, he was taken to the hospital. They figured I could talk to him and try to help him if I came.

I looked everywhere for him before I finally found him. I found him lying in a ditch, just like his mother. I took him to my step-grandmother Mary's house, where she had to clean him up and get him some help. Finding my uncle was one of the hardest things I ever had to do. My uncle died shortly after that. I am glad my mother was able to be with him before he passed. Tony's death sparked some painful memories for everyone because he had such a promising life and had done so much in a short period for Blacks in Lafayette.

Uncle Tony never got to witness what he was most proud of. His sons have all done very well. He had three boys. One became a city councilman in Lafayette, another son is a Louisiana state representative, and his other son is a playwright.

Sports were another passion of mine. When I was seven or eight years old, I played flag football. I was a good football player. As I got older, I started playing other sports. I started pursuing baseball, basketball, track, and wrestling. I was involved in almost every sport. I thrived and lettered in football, track, and wrestling in high school.

My passion for becoming a lawyer changed when I was in college. I started working at a TV station when I was 19. The way it happened was by accident. I knew this young lady who had gone to a different high school. I ran into her at the university and asked her out. She said yes and asked if I would pick her up from her job. I agreed to pick her up and asked where she worked. She told me she worked at the local TV station. When I picked her up, the News Director recognized me because I had played high school football with her son.

After a short conversation, she asked me if I wanted a job, and I said yes. Thus, my career was born.

After I had worked at the TV station for two weeks, one of the reporters, who is now in Chicago, said you need to be a photographer. I said, cool, I can do that. However, I didn't know anything about being a photographer. I had to ask coworkers what a photographer does. Ironically, the chief photographer who hired all the photographers lived two streets from my parents when I was in high school. Therefore, he knew who I was because I played sports. He said, "Oh, that's June Labbe's boy, come here." He taught me how to be a photographer. I started going out and doing news stories, and that's when I quickly realized I had an outstanding News Director, Jan Stratton. I love that lady. She was great. She taught me a lot about the importance of community and how to respect your community regarding journalism. She pushed for the station to be involved in the community. Many TV stations frequently discuss the negatives and dwell on that, but she accentuated the essence of solution journalism. She taught me not to point out the problems in the community. She taught me to find solutions. So, that is what I did. I found issues, told stories, and helped people. I was a photojournalist going out with the reporters and shooting videos. In my mind, I thought, maybe this is something I can do as a career. But I kept going to school while I worked. At one point, it hit me. Do you know what? I can do this. Journalism is the only career I've ever had since I was 19. If I got fired tomorrow, I wouldn't know what to do.

Initially, my job was to run one of those big studio cameras. My job title was called "grip." I gripped everything, like cameras, tripods, and dollies. I was hired as a part-time grip, and then they asked me to be a photojournalist. I loved being a photojournalist, and I flourished at it. It was an incredible job. I enjoyed taking pictures. I enjoyed going out when there was nothing there. For television, it's a visual medium. So, the critical part of telling a story is shooting the visuals and the sound. I think people forget that. You must capture those moments when a door slams or a person yells. Those kinds of things are crucial when telling and writing a story. I love to take pictures and combine the writing with the pictures to make a complete story.

I eventually became a reporter. I did the weather, but I wouldn't say I liked it. I loved going out, taking pictures and sound, coming back, editing, and putting everything together. My coworkers would laugh at me because I would hum when editing and rock back and forth. After all, I loved my job. It was all a flow. I loved creating something out of nothing. I loved being a photojournalist more than I did a reporter because being on TV was never a goal for me.

I had a coworker who loved to share this story about me. I worked 36 hours in a row during hurricane coverage. While I was editing the story, I fell asleep three times. I would doze off, wake up, keep going, and fall asleep again, then wake up and start editing like I never stopped. I loved my craft so much that I built a rhythm over the years. This was more than a job for me; it was an art form.

My Family

I will share some background on my family, starting with my immediate family members. I met my wife through a reporter who works with me. She set us up on a blind date. When we met, I had been divorced for nine years and was not looking to remarry. I didn't know how the date would go, so I took her to an upscale sports bar. I figured if the date didn't work, I could watch basketball since it was during the NBA playoffs. As it turned out, my wife loves basketball. We enjoyed each other's company so much that we watched basketball at the restaurant until it closed. That first date led to a two-year courtship and then marriage.

We have four children. I had two before marrying my current wife, and my wife had two before we got together. We have three boys and one girl, ages 18, 21, 23, and 33. They will tell you my mantra: your family is the most important thing. I push them always to continue to learn and forge their path. Honesty and integrity are fundamental principles that I swear by.

I'm one of those old-school dads. I have open, honest conversations with them. They come to me to talk because they know I will not sugarcoat anything and tell them when they are wrong. They also know I will provide solutions. I walk them through the X, Y, and Zs of situations. On the positive side, I let them know when they do well in certain situations. I usually reach out to them once a week. Getting them to understand they control their destiny has been essential to me. I taught them to ensure they do not let anyone control their actions and to be proactive and not reactive. We just had a couple of funny situations not too long ago. My middle son has a hard time expressing himself to my wife. He once told my wife, "I can talk to Blaise, but it's hard to talk to you." My daughter and wife were talking, dragging me into the conversation. I gave them a suggestion, and my daughter said, "I need more of those. It would help if you interjected more in the conversation."

When it came to discipline, I hardly ever spanked my kids. I was the kind of person who laid out the expectations. I would discipline them when they got older by taking their stuff away, such as video games or cars.

My oldest son was very much into sports, but I needed to teach him that school was also important. Once, I wouldn't let him play in a basketball game to punish him when he flunked a test. But I took him to the game to teach him a lesson by making him see what he missed.

My mom's name is June Rochelle Thomas. My mom's family is originally from San Francisco but moved to Lafayette, Louisiana before I was born. My mom's family was very close, all the way around. My Mom and I have always been and still are very close. My mom was a nurse for 40 years.

I don't know much about my mom's dad, but I do know he died in a hotel fire in San Francisco before I was born. There have always been questions about my maternal grandmother's death because no one knows for sure what happened to her. She was walking to the store or somewhere, and later, she was found dead in a ditch. This happened before I was born, so I didn't get to know her. I didn't know my dad's father. He, too, died before I was born, and I didn't know my paternal grandmother until I was 18.

My mom's great-aunt's name was Mary Martinez. We called her T-Mama. She was the glue that held the family together. She was a tiny lady, probably about 5 feet, 3 or 4 inches tall, and rail thin. She was a very dark-skinned lady with lots of gray hair. Her hair was long, but she would roll it up in a bun. One of T-Mama's most remarkable qualities was her spirit, which stuck out the most about her. She was fiercely loyal to her family. She loved her family, and she would do anything for her family. She was quick to want to fight if somebody did something or said something about our family. She would be the first one out of the door to face them and set them straight. When I was a young boy, we had to stop her from fighting another family member when she was in her seventies.

We were a very Catholic family, so we didn't eat meat on Fridays. We were at my other extended family's house across the street. They gave me some chicken or some other type of meat. Boy, T-Mama was so mad. She was ready to beat up the world. She grabbed a big old rolling pin and headed across the street to beat up my other great-great aunt, Mrs. Moda, for giving me that chicken on a Friday. She was so immensely protective of our family.

T-Mama's daughter's name was Anna Mae Deverges. She is my great-aunt, but I called her grandma. She was probably about 5 feet, 6 or 7 inches tall. She was a little heavyset, portly lady, and very strong. She was built tough, but she had a great big heart. She would stop

T-Mama, her mother, by just talking to her. I can't re-member her being angry about anything. She was al-ways reasonable when it came to issues and conflicts. She was great at talking through issues or problems. She was quick to solve problems. She was the peace-maker, problem solver, and solution person if anything happened. Everyone came to her because she was very wise for her age. She always seemed to have the cor-rect answers needed to solve problems. She was dark-skinned, and her hair was starting to gray. She had a tough exterior. She lived a hard life, probably contribut-ing to her being such a powerful woman with a strong personality. These two ladies were my rock and helped build the foundation for who I am as a man today. I didn't realize it then, but I look back now, and their personal-ities melded and shaped my convictions and character.

I'd like to share a funny story about my mom and great aunt Anna Mae, who bought my mother a pair of new tennis shoes. My mom had made the cheerlead-ing squad, and she wanted to make sure no one picked on my mom for not having any decent shoes to wear. Because my mom had new shoes, she cut holes in the brand-new shoes so people wouldn't make fun of her for having new shoes, which would have led to her getting into fights. It partly worked for my mom. She didn't get into any fight, but my great aunt Anna Mae whipped her butt for tearing up a brand-new pair of shoes.

My mother took on many traits of my great-aunt. She is about 5 feet 6 or 7 inches tall and skinny. She's only about 120 pounds. She is a beautiful, brown-skinned woman. She is very well-spoken, intelligent, and driven. What my mom instilled in us, her kids, came from her being so driven. She was very kind, loving, and nurturing when we were kids. But man, if you crossed her, she would rip you a new one. She had that streak in her that let you know, don't cross her unless you are willing to face the consequences. She took on a little bit of T-Mama's traits, too. She was fiercely loyal to her kids. And boy, if somebody said something or did something wrong to one of her kids, she was in their face and ready to fight.

My father's parents are from Lafayette, also. Edward and Annie Sonnier. They had ten children, seven girls and three boys. My father, Earl Sonnier, was the third boy and baby of the family. My grandmother loved my father; Earl was her favorite. My dad's nickname was T-Cat, meaning "little cat" in Creole. You say T-Cat, and older people would say, "Yeah, we know T-Cat." He was a character. My father died when he was 25 years old.

He committed suicide. Since I was adopted, the Sonnier name stopped at that point because my last name became Labbe. So, our Sonnier family name ended when my father died. It bothered my grandmother that I didn't carry his name; we rarely discussed it. But she made references to me at times about it.

My uncle Tony (my mom's brother) and dad got along well. They both had very magnetic personalities, and people gravitated to them. My dad was very strong-willed. People didn't mess with him. He was a tough man and streetwise. He did his fair share of scraping. People wouldn't mess with him because it was not a good idea. He had a big heart, and that matched his big personality. He was doted upon as the baby in such a large family.

The Issue of Race

It seems that the issue of race has always been intertwined with my life. I was only three years old when James Earl Ray assassinated Dr. Martin Luther King Jr. I don't know how, but I remember I was sitting on the porch and noticed that people were crying and very upset as they walked by. The TVs were on, and I could hear people nearby with their radios turned up extremely loud. I remember hearing my mom crying. She was sitting on the floor. She was very emotional and just crying her heart out. I went to hug her, and I asked her what was wrong. She told me a great man died today. I asked her, "Who was it? Who died?" She said, "You don't know him and wouldn't understand because you're too young." I said, "Well, tell me who died." She said, "A great man." I asked her again, and she told me it was Martin Luther King Jr. She said, "I know you don't know who he is, son." I said, "Yes, I do. He's the man who made it so Black people could eat in restaurants."

As I mentioned, my uncle Tony got involved in

politics, and I remember him fighting for civil rights for Blacks. This made me more conscious of what was happening at a young age. But I only partially understood everything that happened during that era.

In Louisiana, where I grew up, the only White people I knew were the White people I saw on TV because everybody was Black where we lived. When I say everybody was Black, I mean everybody, including the milkman, taxicab drivers, the doctor we went to, and if you died, the funeral home director was Black. The man who owned the grocery store that we went to was Black. He was very light-skinned, and it turned out that he was my great-uncle. The nuns at the Catholic school that I went to when I was a young kid were Black. From birth to age five, that was my world.

Growing up, I saw prominent Black business people doing well. That was my foundation. I grew up with a strong foundation of good, intelligent Black people. They owned businesses, were in the medical field, and knew how to hustle. My mom taught me that Black people were no worse or better than White people. She taught me I needed to understand who I am, meaning I'm Black and intelligent. I was taught this from the time I was a little boy. Mr. Richard owned a grocery store. I was told, "You see that store, you can own a grocery store too. You see Mr. Pat, he's the milkman. He has his own business. Mr. Kinchen owns the funeral home." I can't remember the doctor's name, but he was a Black doctor, so I was told I could also be a Black doctor. I was told I could be whatever I wanted to be.

When I was probably five, I went with my great aunt Anna Mae, whom I called Grandma, to her job as a domestic worker (a maid). She worked for a prominent White family in Lafayette. They had a big old Southern antebellum home. When I first saw the house, I was like, whoa! Compared to the three-room shotgun house I grew up in, it was like a mansion. The family loved my great-aunt and treated Anna Mae well.

That day at work, I asked her, "Hey, grandma, can you come out and play with me?" She was peeling shrimp and said, "No, I have to finish peeling these shrimp, then I have to cook dinner for the family." I said, "Well, can you stop for a bit? Why don't they cook their food themselves? You cook your food when we're at home." I didn't realize that was her job. I didn't know that's what she did for a living.

When I was two, the family she worked for told my great-aunt that since she didn't have money to send my mom to college, they wanted her to take over for my great-aunt and work for them as their maid. My mom refused, so my great-aunt said no. This happened in the late 1960s when the show *Julia* aired on TV. The show *Julia* was the first weekly series to star an African American woman in a non-stereotypical role, but as a professional, she played a nurse. The show inspired my mom to become a nurse.

My great aunt, Anna Mae Deverges, saved the money to pay for my mom to attend nursing school. She didn't make much money working as a maid, but she wanted my mom to get a well-paying job in a profession and not become a maid, so she made the sacrifice to pay for her nursing school. It wasn't until we moved away from Lafayette that we faced racism for the first time. I remember when I was six or seven years old, White people treated us differently. We had moved to Killeen, TX. My dad was in the army and stationed at Fort Hood. If we traveled from Killeen back to Lafayette, there were certain places we couldn't stop to get gas or eat because we were not allowed into those establishments. I remember my parents being very conscious of and talking about that.

When I was 18 years old, I decided to go to the

University of Oklahoma with a couple of other guys to take my college entrance exam. We were wrestling and football teammates. One of the guys was a close friend. After the testing, we decided to save time by getting off the turnpike and taking a back road to get back home. We had to pass through a little town, Marlow, Oklahoma, about 30 minutes from where we grew up in Lawton, Oklahoma. We were all hungry, so we stopped at a Dairy Queen. I stayed in the car. The other guys, two White guys, went inside. It was faster to go inside because they could get in and out quicker than using the drive-through window.

I ordered a Coke float. After they came out of the Dairy Queen, my friend, who I played football with and wrestled with, took the spoon and ate ice cream from my Coke float. I forgot where we were. When I was in high school in 1983, the town of Marlow had a giant billboard at the entrance of the city that said, "When the sun goes down, all niggers leave town." Not think-ing, I got out of the car and said, "Dude, give me my Coke float." He had a banana split or a sundae. I grabbed his spoon and started eating while we were sitting there laughing. An old White lady walked up to me and spit in my face. Then she slapped my friend and said, "I can't believe you're eating after that Nigger." My friend blew up and started yelling and screaming at the lady. I had to pull him away to stop him from doing something I knew he would regret later. He said, "Dude, you aren't pissed?" I said, "Yeah, I'm pissed, but what are we going to do? This is who she is, and we aren't going to get anywhere by arguing with her. We're going to get in trouble. Let's get the hell out of here." So, we left, and that bothered me.

I once dated a young lady who was White. When her family found out, they were not happy that their daughter was dating a Black guy. One day, her dad brought her to my house and told her to make sure I came outside because he was going to shoot me. When he showed up in his pickup truck, he made her leave the pickup truck and come to our front door. When I saw her, she was crying. I asked her, "What's wrong?" She said, "Don't come out! Don't come out!" Then she told me what was going on. My dad overheard what she told me, and he said, "That's it!" And my dad went to get his 12-gauge shotgun out of the closet. He goes, "I'm going to shoot that asshole." My mom grabbed the young lady and brought her into the house. My dad went out with his gun, and I thought there was going to be some shooting, but her dad backed off and drove away.

As a high school sophomore, I had two incidents in Choctaw, Oklahoma. We went there to play football and when we got off the bus, the people there were malicious. They called us all kinds of names. They called us almost every name in the book, such as niggers and jigaboos. They were pointing at us. It was horrible.

The coaches had told us to be careful when we got off the bus and entered the locker room. Walking to the field was like something out of the Twilight Zone. It was 1981, but it felt like we were in the 1950s. The racial slurs and the stares of the people as we walked on the field were hostile. We were told to make sure we kept our helmets on. We had to stand away from the sidelines during the football game because the White fans were standing behind the fence yelling at us. I can't tell you how we won the game, but we won the game. As we left the field, they started throwing rocks at us. They pelted our buses with rocks as we left the stadium.

Then, in 1983, in the same town, we were in a wrestling competition. Another school, an all-Black school from Oklahoma City, Douglas High School, was wrestling in the competition. One of the White guys from Choctaw choked a Black kid from Douglas High School.

He almost broke his neck, and the kid was laid out. His brother, who was also on the team from Douglas High School, went after the White kid while the Choctaw kid's father and brother ran onto the mat. It was a melee of White folks going after teenage Black kids. It seemed like the whole gym converged on the wrestling mat, trying to beat up these Black kids. The police had to come in and separate them, but the police were hitting the Black kids, too. Many of my teammates, both Black and White, were pissed at what we were seeing. So we rushed onto the mat to help the Douglas kids out. Our coaches had to pull us back and remind us that we would be wrestling next in the competition against the Choctaw team.

Those are some instances of racism that I experienced when I was growing up. I guess racism was a part of life growing up in the South then. Little did I know that race would also play a significant role in my life, and it would have nothing to do with anyone of a different skin color.

The Paper Bag
Principle

My mom is brown-skinned. There is a long-held tradition in the Black community in the South called the paper bag principle. Light-skinned Blacks didn't want to mix with darker-skinned Blacks. It was a class system set up from the days of slavery. This principle or tradition started when slave masters had light-skinned enslaved people who worked inside the house and dark-skinned slaves who worked in the fields. So, that skin color or class distinction drove a wrench between the two.

According to the paper bag principle, lighter-skinned Blacks fell into the trap of believing they were superior and wanted their light skin to be a prominent feature in their family. If you were Black and darker than a paper bag, you were not welcomed most times in societal circles of the Black establishment. As time went on through the generations, light-skinned Blacks believed this to be a birthright, and the skin tone needed to be maintained to keep the family legacy.

The paper bag principle is part of my family's history.

It has been a dark secret that has altered my life. It started with the age-old tale of two young kids falling in love: my mother and father, June Thomas and Earl Sonnier. My dad was the ruggedly handsome tough guy, and my mom was the high school cheerleader—what some would call the perfect match. But there was a huge problem; you see, in my dad's family, all of his brothers and sisters were very light-skinned and could pass for White. And well, my mother was brown-skinned and the shade of a paper bag. The long-established tradition of segregation and separation among Blacks based solely on skin tone was about to wreak havoc on two families and two kids.

My mom and dad decided they wanted to get married when she finished high school. My mom was only a senior; they were in love, and the families seemed to accept their dating. But when the discussion of marriage came into play, a cold reality set in. My father's family's truth came out as the family was vehemently opposed to the marriage. Earl's aunt, who is my grandmother's sister and also a nun, led the opposition to my dad and mom's being together. She forbade him to marry my mom. The ironic thing is this was a double standard, as all my aunts married dark-skinned men. Since my dad was the youngest, she didn't want him to marry my mom because the lighter skin tone would be stained; thus, the Sonnier name would suffer because our family's paper bag principle would have been sullied.

Like foolish kids, my parents decided to defy my dad's family wishes, and my mom got pregnant with me on purpose to force the families to change their minds. My grandmother intervened, and there was some give on my dad Earl's side of the family, but not my mother's. Grandma and T-mama said, "No, she wasn't good enough before, so she's not good enough now." We're going to take the baby and raise the baby. This set off a traumatic chain of events.

The families made a pact that my mom and dad should go their separate ways and find other people. My grandmother (Earl's mom) cared for my mom, and some of my dad's sisters cared for her too. But the Sonnier family was a strong Catholic family, and in the 1960s, you didn't go against the wishes of a nun, so they followed the mandate and moved on.

My mom graduated high school and had me. She began to live her life without my father and raise me as a single mother. As she began to see her life beyond

Fightingville, she enrolled in nursing school.

My parents were distraught over their family's actions but obedient because, in those days, as a child and young adult, you did what you were told. This cut deep because they truly loved each other. It was not easy for them, young parents who wanted to do the right thing but were forbidden to. At that time, people looked down on a woman who had a child out of wedlock and viewed men as worthless for not being there for their children. This weighed on them as they struggled to move on in their lives. They contemplated leaving, but my father had no real job, and my mother was starting nursing school, so that was not an option. Their affection for one another was strong, but their commitment to family and obedience was even more powerful. They compromised and agreed to move past one another if I remained in his life.

My mom would let my dad see me from time to time. I remember going on rides in his car and going to the park. I don't know how I remember when I was 3 or 4, but I am glad those memories are there. I remember he had a portable cassette deck he would keep in his glove box so he didn't have to listen to the radio. I remember sitting in his lap with my hands on the steering wheel, feeling like I was driving. But my mom started dating someone, and my dad didn't come anymore. The memories are important because my mom and dad held to the pact. I never knew the man I took rides with and went to the park with was my father.

My father's family encouraged him to marry a woman who passed the paper bag principle with flying colors. Her name was Mary Jane Sonnier. They were related, like third or fourth cousins. That didn't matter because she, like my family, could pass for being White. Her family encouraged her to marry my dad for the same reasons: to maintain the color tone in the family. They eventually got married, but it was more out of convenience to please their families and not so much for love.

My mom eventually fell in love again and married a man named Leo Labbe. When my dad, Earl, found out my mom married Leo, it hurt him tremendously. My dad and Mary Jane had a daughter, Shelly Marie, whom he loved deeply. My father loved my mom, but now the love of his life was gone, and he became increasingly despondent when he couldn't see me or be around me.

The Dream

From about age 5 to 18, I was haunted by a dream. Though it was a dream, it was clear and vivid. I felt like I was there, reliving an event. I was a little boy in a church, and there were many people there. I was in the back of the church, sitting in a pew.

There was a lady with me. I never saw her face, but I felt like it was my mother, and she was crying. I remember getting up and slowly walking to the front of the church. That walk was always a very long one in my dreams. I held the lady's hand as we walked to the front of the church and the altar.

I remember a casket and people crying, some quietly, some loudly. I remember feeling lost and alone. I didn't know why I was there. I didn't know anyone who had died. Why was the lady I was with so upset? In my dream, I would start to cry because I was confused, and then I would wake up.

Nothing clicked year after year, dream after dream, and I remained confused. It was just a dream but so vivid it bothered me each time it happened. I would be depressed and sometimes scared because I had no context for the dream. I would pray and ask God to help me understand, but nothing.

As a kid, there was no way to formulate the words or make sense of the dream to ask anyone. As I got older, I wondered if it was me in the casket. I wanted it to stop or understand why it kept recurring. I just needed an answer to why this dream was haunting me.

My Stepdad and his Family

As I told you earlier, this man came into my life when I was five. It was strange because I was told this is your father. I knew kids had fathers, but I thought, okay, but where did you come from? Why are you here now? There were many questions. The world I knew changed. It was not me and my mom anymore. I remember the day they were married and when they came home. There was a little party for them. I was introduced to a new grandma and grandpa I had never seen before. I remember thinking my grandmother was not lovely, unlike Anna Mae.

A quick note of reference... I talked about everyone calling me Blaise since I was little. I don't remember ever using my last name from birth until I was five years old. I remember my phone number from when I was three years old, but not my last name. The first time I remember having a last name was when I was six and enrolled in school in Killeen, Texas.

Leo Labbe, my stepfather, was born in Broussard,

Louisiana. He was a military guy. Leo is not very tall of a man, about 5 feet, 7 inches tall. He had a receding hairline early on in life. He is very fair-skinned and has straight hair, like his father. He is not a big man. His build is average, and he doesn't smile or laugh that much. He had, for a man, a resting bitch face. The best way to describe him is that he was a real-life George Jefferson. He always had something sarcastic to say about somebody. He had the same demeanor as George Jefferson, from the TV sitcom, *The Jeffersons*. He wasn't a narcissist like George, but his demeanor was the same as George Jefferson's. Growing up, he was never comfortable with or very accepting of me.

Leo's mother, my step-grandmother's name was Mabel Matthews Labbe. I called her Mama. She was a stout, portly woman like my great-aunt Anna Mae. She was about 5 feet 5 inches tall. She looked more Hispanic than Black. She was very fair-skinned, and she had straight black hair. She wore horn-rimmed glasses like the ones they wore in the 1950s and 60s. She had a powerful personality. She had a gruff demeanor about her. It wasn't until she was in her 90s that I saw her smile and laugh. She regularly had a mean look or manner about her. She was another lady who was protective of her family. She was very guarded. She didn't think she was better than anyone else, but the Labbes were fair-skinned people, and many of the paperback principles I shared applied to how she raised her kids. Leo was the exception when he married my mom.

My step-grandfather, whom I called Papa, was Willis Labbe, Sr. He was very fair-skinned. He had straight white hair. He wore glasses with a large brown or black frame. He was a very well-built man. He was about 5 feet and 9 inches tall. He was a very handsome man. Even as he aged, he was a handsome man. He had a very calm and peaceful demeanor. But when he spoke, it was like E.F. Hutton, and everybody listened because he only talked a few times. When he wanted to make a point, he made his point. He worked with his hands either on a farm when he was younger or fixing things. He was very mechanically inclined.

My stepdad's family was large; there were six kids. His oldest brother was a truck driver, his second oldest brother was a businessman, his sister was an educator, his brother closest to him was a priest, and his baby brother was an educator.

They grew up on a farm and had a strict upbringing. My step-grandfather was a tough man who rarely showed emotion, and my step-grandmother was the disciplinarian. They worked very hard to make a living for their children. They eventually moved from Broussard to Lafayette and Fightingville. They attended the same high school as my mother, Holy Rosary Institute. After high school, Leo was drafted into the army.

Mable was very protective of her kids. Leo was the second youngest and a momma's boy. My uncle, a priest, was the light of her eye, but my stepdad Leo was her boy. I think the fact that he married my mom, a woman who had a child out of wedlock, bothered her. I was that child she had out of wedlock. My step-grandmother was not the kindest person when I was a child. After all, I wasn't one of her blood grandchildren. I don't think my step-grandmother was being mean directly. She felt she was protecting her family, and I wasn't part of the family by blood.

I was extremely close to my cousin, Aquinas Domangue, who, as I talked about earlier, was related to me on my mom's side. Coming from that side of my family, he was dark-skinned. I had mentioned earlier that I would stay at his house when we returned to Lafayette for a visit. One of the reasons I would stay with him was because he was not allowed in the Labbe house. My step-grandfather Willis was born as a product of a rape in 1911. He was the first child born to my great-grandmother. She was a brown-skinned lady, and his father was a White man. Willis was very light-skinned with straight hair. When his mother got older, she married a dark-skinned man. So, my step-grandfather's brothers and sisters didn't look like him, and he was treated differently, not by his mother, but by the family because he was light-skinned and could pass for White. I have come to realize now why my step-grandfather treated me the way he treated me.

He tried to have a close relationship with me because he could relate to me in his way. It was important to him to make me feel part of something, part of a family. Looking back on our time together, I realize he treated me differently than the other grandkids. When the grandkids were over and playing, he always had me sit down and watch TV with him, and I would sit on his lap.

When he went to work in his garage, he always said, "Hey, come with me." I spent a lot of time with him, talking with him and him showing me things he was fixing or working on. When I think about the time we spent together, those times were very special to me because I didn't know all this about him until later in life, but now I realize why my step-grandfather and I had a special connection.

He had a connection with me that was different from what he had with his other grandkids. He knew what happened between my mom's family and my dad's family. He was ostracized as a child because of the paper bag principle. So here I was, growing up not the same way but living in his situation.

My life was not always easy. My stepdad, Leo, and I clashed a lot growing up. I felt like there was always a feeling of emptiness, and he never really fulfilled it. He was a very, very tough man. He went to Vietnam, where he did two tours. I'm not saying he was an alcoholic, but he drank a lot. I think post-traumatic stress disorder (PTSD) was a factor, and I don't think the drinking helped either. I felt almost like he resented me. He would always tell me I was no good and wouldn't make anything out of myself. He probably saw my dad in me because everyone said I looked like him when I was younger. My build is like his, and we have the same facial structure.

He was both physically and mentally abusive to me. My mom and Leo had two children: my younger sister Mikula and brother Eric. They didn't escape his wrath, but I was the main target and felt it more harshly.

For me, it was the mental abuse that was the most damaging. He rarely acknowledged or even spoke to me the older I got. When he did talk to me, it was a barrage of beratement. He was cold towards me, never a hug or pat on the back. In his eyes, I was always wrong. Everything I did was wrong; I was stupid, and I was destined to be a bum. This is what I was told daily. Week after week, year after year.

Remember, this was my father; I didn't know any difference. So, it was hard for me to understand as a young child. I was confused and wondered, "Why does my father hate me?" That's what I grew up with. The thought that I had done something wrong always danced inside my head because nothing I did was good enough for him. I excelled in almost everything I did. Whether it was school, grades, or sports, I gave 100 percent. I wish I could say it was for me, but I just wanted and needed his approval.

It motivated me to strive to do bigger and better things. It became adversarial; the more he hated me, the more I wanted to do better and show him up. Once, in the eighth grade, I came home and said, "Guess who's the starting quarterback?" I was staring at him right in the face. I thought he would be proud of me. Starting quarterback is a coveted position in football, even if you're just a kid. I felt like I had ascended into something. But he didn't care one way or the other. He never said great job or congratulations; he just stared back at me.

I taught myself most things that young men usually learn from their fathers, like driving, sports, and fighting. It was tough to see other kids hanging out with their dads. I watched sons with their fathers at sporting events, cheering them on and having someone to talk to about growing up. I learned these things from my friends and their conversations with their dads.

By the time I was a senior in high school, I was class president and president of the largest service organization in school. I was vice president of the Lettermen's Club. I was even voted Mr. MHS at MacArthur High School in Lawton, Oklahoma. You would expect your parents to be proud of these things, but I got nothing. Leo was not impressed and never budged on his belief that I would turn out to be nothing.

Growing up, I accomplished many things that should have instilled confidence, but deep inside, I had an identity crisis. I had self-doubt; I was not good enough and feared failing and becoming what Leo believed I would be nothing.

For me, my life seemed to be in turmoil. I often wondered why my life was a mess and asked God if I had done something wrong. I didn't understand why Leo hated me so much or what I had done to him to make him hate me. I tried so hard to make him proud of me. I was a good student and athlete and a positive example for Mikula and Eric, but nothing was good enough for him. I felt very alone. I had friends and was popular in school, but I still felt like I didn't fit in anywhere.

Sometimes, I would cry, lying on the driveway, looking at the stars. I lived a mile from the junior high school and high school. From seventh grade to my junior year in high school, I would walk home from football and wrestling practice, often fearing coming home. What would I have done today to cause ire? What would I be belittled for, or would I have to fend off physical attacks? That one mile was very long and lonely; many of those walks were filled with tears.

The Truth Revealed

My senior year was a challenging year for me. During football season, I was injured. I took hard hits to my head two weeks in a row. I wound up suffering from a brain contusion. We were at an away game when I had the second blow to the head. It was a long bus ride home. I felt dizzy and nauseous but didn't make the coaches aware; I just figured I would go home to sleep and feel better in the morning. I wound up sleeping most of the next day. I believe I woke up around 4 pm. I got up for a couple of hours and was still very dizzy and sick to my stomach. I started throwing up and eventually went back to sleep around 7 pm that night. A party was going on since it was Saturday and in the middle of football season. One of my friends came by around 9:30 pm. He talked to my mom, who told him I was in bed. He asked if he could speak to me, she said yes. He came and woke me up and talked me into going out. We went to a gathering of friends, and I passed out. He rushed me home, and I went straight to bed.

The next day was Sunday, and my mom came to wake me up for church. I told her I still felt sick and didn't want to go. Leo was unhappy and said how lazy I had been sleeping all day, but I had time to go to a party. The family left for church, and I went back to sleep. While they were at church, I woke up with a bad headache, and then I began coughing up blood. I was dizzy, and my vision became blurry. I knew something was wrong and was scared, so I took our other car and drove to the hospital. While at the hospital, I was diagnosed with a brain contusion. The doctors called our house and told my parents what was going on. My mom is a nurse and talked to the doctor when they arrived. When she finished, she spoke to Leo to explain what was happening. As I lay in the hospital bed, I could hear him tell my mom how pissed he was that I drove the car to the hospital. I could have wrecked his car, and then what? Here I was in the hospital, bleeding in my brain, and my father was concerned about his car and not me. It was a heartbreaking moment for me. I thought this was what I got for not going to church. I was so scared knowing that I had bleeding in my brain, and then to hear what Leo said, that was the first time I thought about committing suicide.

Fortunately, the contusion healed without any surgery. I missed the last four football games and the playoff game. I was able to wrestle that year and had a pretty good season. However, throughout the year, there was one conflict after another with Leo. I remember coming home from school one day around 6:30 pm after wrestling practice. I sat at the table to start doing my homework, and Leo said, "Did you pick it up?" I asked, "What?" he said, "The milk jug in the yard." I said, "Sorry, I didn't see it." It was December, and it was dark outside. He began to cuss me out and call me names. He told me I was stupid and nasty and that I liked living in garbage. I got up, went into the front yard, and picked up the milk jug from the middle of the yard. I had to look for it because it was dark.

These are just a few of the issues I lived with during my last year in high school. In May and the final weeks of school, things got very strenuous between Leo and me. I had to attend an award banquet with him because my mom couldn't make it. I was representing my high school, something most parents would have been proud of, but Leo was agitated that he had to attend. We didn't talk on the way there and didn't talk while there or on the way home. On graduation night, it was the same; there was no conversation whatsoever. This led to a heated discussion between us a few days later.

The month of June was hectic. I had 17 scholarship offers. I wasn't a great athlete, but a good one. I was trying to weigh all the options and the various aspects of what I wanted to do. Toward the end of June, I signed a letter of intent to go to a small school in Colorado, Adams State University, on a wrestling scholarship. I was excited about the opportunity to wrestle while attending college. It gave me something to take my mind off what was happening in my family life. I felt like I had some direction. The scholarship would only pay for some things since Adams University has a small student population. Since Leo had a GI Bill, I thought he and my mom would use that to help cover the other college costs not covered by the scholarship.

One morning in July, we were getting ready to go to a 40-year reunion for Leo. Leo and I got into a huge fight because he told me he would not use his GI Bill to help me attend college. He left the house after the fight, and I told my mom I hated him. I asked her, "What does he want from me?" I had been a good kid, someone he could be proud of, but he hated me. I asked my mom, "What did I do to make him hate me so much?"

My mother asked me to sit down with her at the kitchen table. She started crying and said, "It is time I told you the truth." I didn't know what was coming, but I was frozen. She said the words that would send me into shock and rage. *"Leo is not your father".*

I was furious, and many things began to swirl in my head. My mother went on to explain that there was a house we would go to when we visited Lafayette from time to time. There was an older lady there, and there were some kids at that house I had played with growing up who were my cousins; she named a couple of ladies that I remembered and told me they were my aunts. The more she explained, the more my anger quickly turned into outrage and just pure hatred toward my mom.

I asked why she had waited until now to tell me and why she had allowed Leo to treat me like he had. She told me she wanted to protect my younger brother and sister and keep the family together. She prayed that I would be strong enough to take it.

It was not enough for me to discover that the man I thought was my father was not my father. But suddenly, I found that there were people who had been in my life and were my family, and I didn't know it. To make things worse, my mother told me that I had a sister, and she believed her name was Shelly; she didn't know much about her, but she lived on the West Coast. I was devastated. All I could do was cry; it felt like my soul had left my body, and I was a shell. I was confused about where my father was and why he hadn't contacted me. My mother explained then that he had committed suicide. My mom told me that after my father's death, the families entered a pact to keep me and my sister separated. Then, I started to connect the dots and realized that my father was the man who would come and get me and take me on those drives and to the park. This is why we would visit the old lady's house, which was my grandmother's.

But then I felt paralyzed because the next revelation was the answer I most dreaded. My dream was the dream that had haunted me for thirteen years. It was all a reality: the church, the lady crying, the long walk to the casket. I finally knew who was in the casket; it was my father.

Meeting the Sonniers

In July, when the time came, we took a trip to Lafayette, Louisiana, from Lawton, Oklahoma. My mom called and talked to her brother, my uncle Tony, and shared with him that she had finally told me the truth. She asked my uncle to help me with whatever I needed and explain the situation and the circumstances regarding what happened. She thought it would be best if he took me to meet my grandmother.

I had planned to stay with my cousin Aquinas. When we arrived, they dropped me off at his house and went to my grandmother Mable and Papa Willis's home. My instructions were that I needed to be prepared to join them again later in the week because they were planning on having a family reunion..

The next day, after we arrived in Lafayette, my uncle Tony came to my cousin's house and said he was taking me for a haircut. We went to the barbershop, and he said, "Hey, I want you to look nice when you meet your grandmother, and we need to have that conversation."

So, we both got a haircut, and he talked about my dad and how he admired him. He said my dad had taught him a lot because he was younger than my dad. He asked, "Well, when do you want to meet your grandmother?" I said, "Give me a couple of days," and he said, "Nope, you're going to go today." I said, "I don't know if I'm ready to do all this." He said, "Well, you're going to get ready. There's no time like the present, so go back home, relax, and think about what you want to say. Be prepared to have a conversation." So, I went to my cousin's house and talked to him. I shared everything that had happened with him, and lo and behold, he said, "Oh yeah, we all knew." He was only two years older than me but swore not to say anything. It was a shock at how many people knew that Leo wasn't my biological father. We're talking now about an extended part of the family, and nobody said anything. I had to contemplate all that and try to get it to make sense.

My uncle called me later and said he had some things to do but would pick me up around one that afternoon. He picked me up and said, "Okay, I will drop you off. Stay as long as you need, and call me when you're ready for me to pick you up." Then he changed his mind and said, "Okay, I don't want to put that much pressure on you." He said, "I'm going to drop you off, and I'm going to come back and pick you up in about an hour or hour and a half." I said okay, and then we drove to my real grandmother, Annie Sonnier's house. It was one of the most challenging days I've ever had.

I remember walking up the steps to the front door. I was so scared I was trembling. I didn't know what was going to happen. I didn't expect my grandmother to know who I was. I didn't know how she would react when I told her who I was. I was terrified, to be honest, about rejection, so I stood in front of the door for probably five, maybe even 10 minutes, before I knocked on the door. At some point, I gathered enough muster and knocked on the door.

A few minutes later, the door opened, and this old lady looked at me for two to three minutes and began to cry. I didn't know what to do, so I cried, too. I didn't expect her to recognize me or know who I was. After crying, she hugged me and said, "Please come in." I said, "I need to tell you something." I told her, "I'm your grandson." She said, "I know who you are; please come in." I entered the house, and that moment was awkward, but the awkwardness was not bad. We didn't know what to say to one another. She asked me to sit down in a chair.

She sat in a recliner, and my chair was close to her recliner. She just sat there and held my hand. I don't know how long we just sat there and looked at each other.

Finally, she asked me, "Are you hungry?" I said I wasn't hungry, and she said, "No, no, no, no, you need to eat," and that's the way we broke the ice. Then she got up and fixed me a plate of food like every grandmother would do for their grandchild. We sat at the table and made small talk about nothing. I didn't want to ask a bunch of questions. I didn't want to return to the moment at the front door. I just wanted to absorb that moment. I just wanted to be in her presence. It was a love that I can't tell you I had felt before, or to be honest, since my grandmother Anna Mae.

This time spent with my grandmother, Annie Sonnier, was the first time I felt that same way. I felt connected. I just wanted to be in the moment. We just talked and laughed. She asked questions about my little sister and brother. She knew about my siblings Mikula and Eric.

She asked about my mom and how she was doing. She asked me questions about school. I told her I was getting ready to go to college and was going to play sports in college. She was so excited. We talked for about an hour, or maybe even longer. She asked me how long I was going to be there. I told her I would be there for a few days and asked if it was okay if I came back again. She said, "Yes, I want you to come back because there are things we need to discuss." I said, "Great, I appreciate it." By then, my uncle had shown up to pick me up, so I left. I was so excited to talk to her again, so I returned to her house the following day. The lady I remembered from childhood who lived across the street came over and introduced herself. She said," Hey, I don't know if you remember me, but I'm Nora, your aunt." I said, "I remember you." But I knew her as Miss Jolivette, not as my Aunt Nora.

They called my dad's other sisters over to my grandmother's house. My Aunt Gertrude, whom they called Tuddy, my Aunt Earline, Aunt Teresa, the oldest sibling, and Sister Ann Elise, my aunt who was a nun, came over. I was introduced to all of them on the second day I visited my grandmother. We didn't get into many details about a lot of things. It was a rough situation because my father had committed suicide in a bedroom in the house.

My grandmother would not go into that bedroom after he killed himself. They explained those things, but they never really got into the other parts of what exactly happened to my dad. There are different stories about what happened the night my father committed suicide. But no one has discussed in detail what happened, just that it happened.

I asked about my sister, and they told me a little about her and her mom, Mary Jane. They told me they were living in California. My Aunt Teresa was the oldest and the boss. She said, "You know what, we need to call Mary Jane. So, we went next door to my Aunt Nora's house. They picked up the phone and called Mary Jane. They told her, "Blaise knows what's going on. He's here, and we've been talking to him." They said it was time for Shelly and me to meet. They asked Mary Jane if she would be willing to let Shelly come. To Mary Jane's credit, she didn't hold back. I think my sister Shelly was on a plane the next day. It was on a Wednesday because it seemed to be in the middle of the week. I remember we all met Shelly at the airport. It was cool. We have a great picture of all of us together at the airport.

They had bottles of champagne, and it was a grand celebration. It was somewhat awkward because I knew Shelly was my family; however, I didn't know her as family. We all met at my Aunt Nora's or maybe my grandmother's house. We sat and briefly talked because she didn't arrive until late afternoon or evening. We said we would get together the next day. It was kind of like, wow, it was a whole different world. My life was starting to feel like this was how things should be. It was a very exciting and magical time for me.

Shelly and I had a chance to talk the next day. We went to my godfather's house because he and my dad were very close. We talked, and he shared things with us. He took us to our dad's gravesite. That was the first time I had visited my dad's gravesite. It was very emotional. I don't remember when exactly we got there. It may have been on a Sunday. It was a fantastic feeling because, by Thursday, my whole world had changed. I had a whole new family of aunts, uncles, and cousins. The crazy thing again is that those cousins were people that I had grown up playing with (Keith, Byron, Doug), but I never knew they were my family.

At that point, so many things were going on in my head. It was the craziest thing. I had given the coach from Adams State University my phone number because they wanted us to get there early to start training. I told him what was happening with my family and asked if I could have more time. He was very accommodating.

I'm learning all these new things: people's faces,

names, and new family members. It was a wonderful, wonderful experience. In the meantime, my mom and Leo were preparing for the barbecue at the 40-year high school reunion. By the time I got there, it was a lot different. It was cold. I had gone a few times to see the Labbe side of the family. Leo and I didn't talk, but that was nothing unusual. We went to the barbecue, and it was weird because I felt so estranged. We put on the happy family facade that everything was great even though it wasn't.

I felt so isolated watching the other kids interact with their parents. I had no attachment to my own family at that point. I'm not going to lie; it was terrible after experiencing what I was experiencing and coming back into that atmosphere. I hated them for putting me through all of this. I hated them for all of this to have happened. I kept going back to my childhood. The question began again to rage, "What did I do to deserve this? Why me?" I didn't want to be a part of any of that.

It was tough trying to grasp everything that had transpired. I was so angry at my mom and Leo that I didn't consider the role the Sonniers played in all of this. I had a wall up because of the hurt. At the time, I just wanted to belong to a family, something I never fully experienced. I felt like I was part of the Labbe family but never truly belonged. There was confusion and apprehension with the Sonnier clan, but I opened myself up to them mainly because of the love my grandmother Annie gave me. She calmed my confusing world, and I felt better being with her. We filled a giant void in each other's lives. Looking back on how angry I was, some of my anger should have been directed at the Sonnier family because they partly orchestrated what my life had become.

My New Reality

When we had to return to Oklahoma, I asked if I could stay a little longer to spend some time with Shelly. At that point, Leo knew that I knew, and I was trying to get to know my other family. My mom and Leo agreed that I could stay a little longer. I don't remember how I got back to Oklahoma. I stayed another week or so. I was so excited about that experience. It was even more exciting because I had called the coach and said, "Hey, I'm going back to Oklahoma. I need to get myself together, and then I will be ready to start working." He said, "We're looking forward to you being here, and sure enough, by the time I returned to Oklahoma, my world crashed again. I came home, and they had put everything I owned in boxes. Leo was there waiting for me. He told me I had two weeks to get out. Leo said, "I don't care where you go, but you have two weeks to leave." He said they weren't going to help me with college.

I was beyond devastated, knowing that I was being kicked out of the house and knowing there'd be no help with paying my college tuition. I can't begin to tell you how devastated I was. I was so disillusioned and thought, here we go again. This compounded the situation I was already dealing with, meaning a family I didn't know about and, especially, a father I didn't know about. These were all the things I didn't ask for, but now I had to find a way to deal with them. I felt like I just kept getting punched in the gut. I don't know how to explain it, but it was making me feel like screaming, "Why was I even born? What was wrong with me? Why did these things keep happening to me?" So, I got myself together and loaded my car with what I could fit in it.

I drove back to Louisiana. My grandmother couldn't take me in, so I asked a cousin if I could stay with her, and she said yes. I stayed with my cousin, Stephanie Labbe, Leo's niece. She was his oldest brother's daughter. This was quite a strange time in my life.

My uncle Tony had become a school board member then. He was very prominent in Lafayette politics. He helped me get enrolled in school. I enrolled and started school at what is now the University of Louisiana, Lafayette. But when I went to school there, it was the University of Southwest Louisiana. I was fortunate because on my real dad's side, one of my aunts worked at the university, and Leo's sister's husband, my uncle Clayton, who I loved and adored to death, was a professor there. He was the dean of education. He was the first Black dean of a college at the university. Enrolling in that school and having family members working there was great. It was helpful as I made this difficult transition in my life.

As time began to pass, I found out that depression was a real thing and very deep in the Sonnier family. I was no different, and I fell into an intense depression myself during that time. I was so unhappy. At one point, I had a severe nervous breakdown and had to be hospitalized. Not long after being released from the hospital, I was drawn back to where I grew up on Washington Street. I would leave campus at night and go back to the house I grew up in. I would sit on the front porch until two or three o'clock, doing nothing.

I would think about killing myself. I didn't want to be alive anymore. I started to hate myself. I hated who I was because I couldn't understand why these things had happened to me. One night, I had a knife, and I thought about stabbing myself to death with it. I was thinking, well, my father killed himself, so what's the big deal? I can't tell you what stopped me. It probably didn't help the situation that I'd started drinking heavily. You know, at the young age of 18, out of 24 hours in a day, I may have been sober for only 4 of those hours. It was an awful time for me.

I didn't realize it at the time, but even as a kid, I lived in a state of depression. I didn't know anything about depression, but I look back and think about it. I always felt alone and felt so empty.

Sitting on that porch, I would think about my childhood and high school. Looking back, God blessed me with a couple of angels. I had a couple of coaches who inspired me and helped me emotionally. I never told anyone what was happening at home, but it seemed they knew. One of my coaches, Kenny McSwain, lived in my neighborhood, so he knew me beyond just playing sports. He instilled confidence in me and helped me find pride in myself. The other coach was Henry Dirickson.

We called him Coach D. I truly loved Coach D. He became a mentor, confidant, and a great advocate. He pushed me past my limits and made me always want to be better. Coach D. and Kenny McSwain are no longer with us, but they were inspirations in my life. They gave me purpose during a difficult time. It was a time I needed and wanted a father, but I didn't have one. I had a provider.

Despite everything, I continued to try to get through college. Not long after, I moved in with my uncle Tony, who, at the time, I didn't know, but he was very heavily into selling drugs. At one point, I was helping run bags of cocaine for him with his customers. It was not a good life for an 18-year-old. I was doing things I probably shouldn't have been doing. Fortunately, I never did drugs, but I constantly got drunk, got into fights, and did all kinds of crazy stuff. I was hoping someone else would end my life instead of me having to do it, considering all of the crap that I was getting into.

The depths of where I had been hurt were the lowest when I lived in Louisiana between the first and second semesters of college. I went back to Lawton over the Christmas holidays. Things were still bad between Leo and me, so I was not allowed to stay home. I was staying at a friend's house. He was not there when I invited two friends to come over. We were all having fun, drinking, and getting drunk. We ran out of liquor, so my friends went to buy some more while I stayed at the house alone. It had been snowing, and there was ice covering everything. I had reached my endpoint. I had broken up with my girlfriend, I could not see my little brother and sister, and it was snowing. I was miserable.

Before my friends left, we talked, and I was sharing how much my life had changed in six months, from having scholarships and a close, meaningful relationship with my girlfriend to having nothing and not even knowing who I was. When my friends left, I started thinking, and it hit me: I didn't have a reason to be on this earth. I was born into a life of lies. Everyone had just abandoned me like an old rag. I sat there for a few minutes and thought about my dad. My friend, with whom I was staying, had several guns in his house. I saw the guns. I pulled one out and put it in my mouth. The door flew open just as I was about to pull the trigger. My friends had slipped off the icy road, and the car was stuck. They returned to the house to get me to help them push the car out of a snow drift. I was startled and froze. My friends were able to grab me and the gun and stop me. I started to cry and kept telling them I wanted to die; timing is everything. I was as low as possible and was spinning entirely out of control.

I returned to Lafayette and college. It's hard to describe everything I was going through during that time. I struggled through school the first semester. Then, I started the second semester doing the same thing I was doing the first semester: constantly drinking. As

I mentioned, I had moved in with my uncle; we didn't have furniture, we didn't have food in the house, but we had cocaine. At one point, I realized I hadn't eaten food for a week and a half. I didn't have money to put gas in my car, so I missed school for four days. It was during a holiday.

The only thing I survived on was water, and for some weird reason, I remember we had candy corn in the house. So, I ate candy corn and drank water. That is what I survived on: candy corn and water. Toward the end of the semester, I was able to scrounge up enough change to get some gas to put in my car.

Mary Chassion was my step-grandmother, and she was Tony's stepmother. She married my mom's step-dad, Alton Chassion Sr. I was very close to her as a little boy and teenager. I spent a lot of time at her house just talking to her. As mentioned, on Fridays and Saturdays, they had intense poker games. She and my step-grand-father always gave me money. There was another reason I loved to go over to their house. My step-grand-mother was a great cook. She was a great lady; even though my mom and uncle were not her biological chil-dren and didn't live with her, she still loved them and was there for them and her grandkids.

After I filled up my car with gas, I went to my step-grandmother Mary's house. When she saw me, she couldn't believe how I looked. I had not eaten much, so I had lost significant weight. When I first started school at the University, I weighed 190 pounds. When she saw me, I lost about 40 pounds and was down to 150. I had lost a tremendous amount of weight because not only was I not eating much, but I was also drinking heavily. She called my mom and said, "You need to get this boy home." She gave me money to put gas in the car, and I drove back to Oklahoma.

Photo Gallery

Biological grandmother and grandfather, Annie and
Edward Sonnier

My mother, June Labbe, and me

Great Aunt Sister Anna Marie, Shelly, and my father,
Earl Sonnier

The couple on the right is our father Earl and Shelly's mom
Mary Jane

Shelly and Blaise

A young Blaise

A young Shelly

My grandmother, Annie Sonnier

My sister Mikula and me

My brother Eric and me

Five of my father Earl's sisters

My father and uncle's headstone

All seven of my fathers sisters

My grandmother Annie Sonnier and my aunt,
Sister Ann Elise Sonnier, My father's sister.

My grandmother Annie Sonnier (second from left sitting), and all her siblings

My sisters Mikula, Shelly, and me

This is the day Shelly and I met for the first time. It was at the Lafayette, LA airport in 1983. With us are our Aunt Savanah, Aunt Sister Ann Elise, and Aunt Gertrude

Induction into the Oklahoma Journalism Hall of Fame

My grandmother Mable Labbe, and my wife Yira Labbe

High School Wrestling

Number 34 High School Football

My mother, June Labbe, and father, Leo Labbe

Being inducted into the Oklahoma Journalism Hall of Fame

My Grandfather, Willis Labbe Sr

Me Chilling in my office

My family

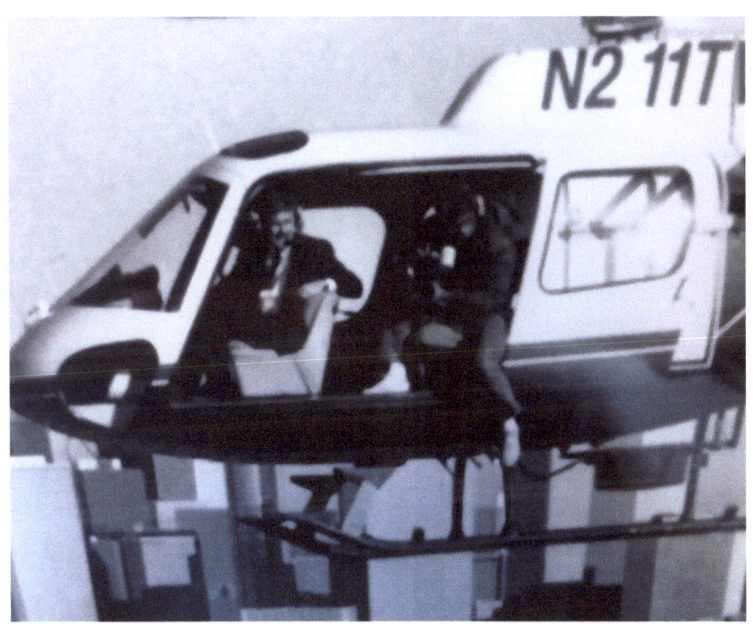

Taking video high over Houston (circa 1993)

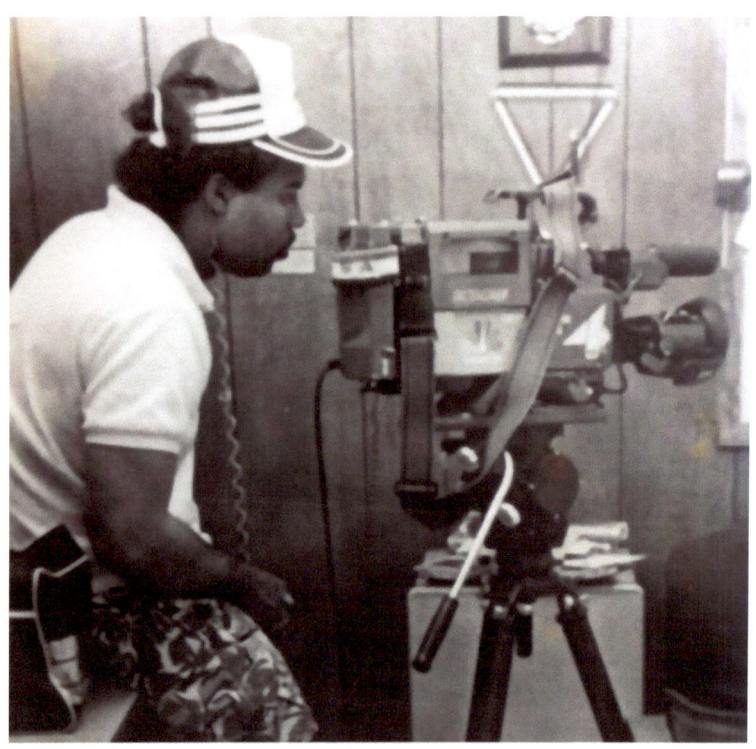
A young photojournalist in Amarillo, TX (circa 1987)

My siblings

God Works His Work

When I got back to Oklahoma, Leo was not there. He was on a tour in Korea. I just hung out the first couple of days after I got home. At that point in my life, my relationship with my mom was very strained. It was the weirdest thing. I went to talk to a friend, a young lady I knew who just happened to work at the local TV station.

We had decided to go out on a Friday night, and I went to pick her up. I met the News Director. I had known her since I was about 14. I played high school football with her son. She had come to the school and spoken several times. She remembered me and asked me what I was doing. After filling her in on what I had been doing, she asked, "Do you want a job?" I was like, "Uh, okay."

I enrolled at Cameron University in Oklahoma. While I was attending school, I started working at the television station. I began to get some of my confidence back. I started to feel good about myself. I was learning something and doing something new. I enjoyed the aspects of being in and working at the TV station. They taught me how to be a photojournalist.

I learned to go out and take pictures with a video camera, do interviews, work with reporters, and learn how to edit. This photojournalist job started a successful career and led me to what I do today.

Returning to Lawton, Oklahoma, and getting this job was more of a blessing than I could ever have known or imagined. Looking back over my life, I see that job became my career and livelihood.

Getting that job put some focus into my life and gave me something to work toward that I was missing. Working in television gave me purpose. Slowly, my mom and I began to work on mending our relationship.

Now, when things started getting better with my mom, Leo was not there. He was still in Korea. I don't remember how long I was back in Oklahoma before Leo came home. It could have been a few months before he returned. Sadly, things were just like they were before. There was much tension. There was anxiety. I mean, not only for myself but for my younger brother and sister. My mom was also anxious because she was the one who tried to keep the peace in the house.

Things had become very contentious because Leo was unhappy that I had moved back home. One afternoon, it seemed God gave me confidence and the right words to say. I asked Leo and my mom if I could talk to them that evening. They agreed, and we gathered at the kitchen table. I explained that I was tired of hurting, mainly because I didn't ask to be born or adopted; I just wanted peace. As hard as it was, I was honest with them. I told my mom I had not fully forgiven her for withholding everything from me. I still had resentment toward her for allowing me to go through what I did growing up. I went on to tell Leo how much I hated him for what he put me through. There were times I wished he was dead. I didn't know if I could ever find forgiveness for how he treated me, Mikula, and Eric. I truly hated him for that.

To their credit, they listened. My mom was visibly upset. Leo did not react, but I felt a different aura coming from him. I told them that If I needed to leave, I would; I just needed time to save enough money to move out. We all left the table and went to bed. Leo asked me how my day was when I got home from work the next day. He engaged me in conversation.

As the weeks went on, we talked more and more.

He got engaged in Mikula and Eric's events in school. Day by day, the tension in our house became less and less. For the first time, we started to gel as a family. I eventually moved out. I got a job in Wichita Falls, Texas. Leo was there to help me move and ensure I was set, helping me register for my home phone, energy, and water bill as this was my first time living independently. Though he never said anything at the kitchen table that night, his actions spoke louder than words.

Since the kitchen table talk, Leo has been there for me, Mikula, Eric, and our kids. Financially and emotionally, as an advocate and a mentor, he has been there for whatever we needed. The man I grew up with is not the man he became. I love the guy. The things we went through brought us together, and now, our relationship is more solid than we could have imagined.

They say God works in mysterious ways, so be kind to people because you may be entertaining angels unaware. I was in my late 20s when a bizarre thing happened. I was working for a TV station in Houston. I was a cameraman shooting a story at the Houston Ship Channel along the docks. There was nobody there but me, and suddenly, a gentleman was standing behind me, and he startled me. He appeared out of nowhere.

When I say he appeared out of nowhere, I mean he appeared out of nowhere. I turned to face him, shook his hand, and said, "Can I help you?" He said, "I just wanted to see you." Then I said, "Excuse me, do I know you?" And he said, "Yes." I stretched my hand to him and said, "I'm Blaise Labbe." And he said, "That's not your name." And I said, "I think you have me confused with somebody else." So, I said, "That is my name. My name is Blaise Labbe." And he said again, "That's not your name." He said, "You're a Sonnier. You're the little Sonnier boy." I was shocked because, at that point in my life, few people knew I was a Sonnier. I said, "Excuse me." He smiled and said "yeah, I know you,". The gentleman began to tell me things about me that were true.

He told me he remembered me when I was three years old. At this time, I was about 28. He told me I grew up on North Washington Street in Lafayette. I used to watch you play. He explained I would visit a man by the name of Mr. Dudley. I don't remember her name, but he knew Mr. Dudley's wife's name. Then he said, "You used to go to their house when you were about three years old and eat orange sherbet ice cream." This weird encounter with a stranger scared me because everything he said was true. I did not know this man. He said he knew the Sonnier family and everything about them." "You know your family has an interesting past, right?" He told me, "Your great, great grandfather had long jet-black hair that came all the way down to his butt. Everybody used to talk about him because he rode a horse from Lafayette to Houston." At that moment, I could only say, "Whoa!"

He also shared another crazy story about my family, which happened when my father was playing in a field, and something occurred to him that caused him to collapse. According to the story, he collapsed because he had stopped breathing. Other people were in or near the field. They started crowding around my father to help him. A lady walked over to him and pushed everybody back. I don't know who she was. I don't think she was related to us. As the story goes, she laid her hands on him and did some weird stuff. She took her hands off of him, then she raised her hands, and his body levitated off the ground. He came back to consciousness and started breathing again. I had heard that story from some of my aunts. I have no clue how he would have known that.

After meeting that man, I struggled with changing my name to Sonnier. I felt his presence had some meaning, and he was trying to show me I was missing something. Was I supposed to carry the Sonnier name on? Did I need to honor my father? I contemplated this for a couple of months. I considered how my life was in order and whether this would upset others. How do I explain this to my young son? I started to get depressed and stressed because I felt lost again in who I was.

After much consternation, God guided me to an answer. Who I was ... was me; the experiences, the hurt, the joy, the anguish, and the love that had been poured into my life made me who I am. I am not a name or a family but a person that the Almighty Himself has shaped. I began to feel a renewed sense of who I was. Whoever I met on the dock that day sparked a change, and I know now that meeting was indeed a blessing.

My Sister Shelly

This story would not be complete without my sister Shelly's side and how her life was affected by the Paper Bag Principle and the family secret. Shelly was three years old when our dad committed suicide, and I was five. She has more vivid memories of him than I do because she lived with him. Losing our dad affected her immensely in her life; Shelly felt a double loss. She longed for an actual father figure and felt a void because she had no brothers or sisters. It was always just her and her mother.

Shelly's mom, Mary Jane, and our dad, Earl, were both Sonniers and distant cousins. Their families encouraged their courtship and subsequent marriage. The bloodline and the purity of the skin color were more important than individuals' love for one another. For Shelly, the Paper Bag principle was there from the start, but in a different way from me.

Our father was the baby of his family. Shelly said that when she listened to stories about our father, they talked about him like a saint or a hero. She knows that the older generation wanted to protect the Sonnier name. They didn't want to tarnish their name, especially after he died. The fact that he wanted to marry a dark-skinned woman who had two children two years apart and one out of wedlock was his secret, as well as the Sonnier's secret. The Sonnier family was bound to keep his secret even after his death, keeping the Sonnier name clean. They loved our father. And since he took his life and wasn't here to tell his true story, they weren't going to let the story be told.

Many families have secrets of this kind. They don't tell them because doing so would damage the family name. My sister believes that's one of the reasons the pact was made, and it was important for the Sonniers to keep us apart and maintain the Sonnier secret.

Growing up, I had a family structure, though a bit dysfunctional. I had a family structure, but Shelly didn't. It was tough because Mary Jane had to leave Shelly alone as she sometimes worked two jobs to make a living for the two of them. Shelly and Mary Jane moved around a lot, and Shelly had difficulty fitting in. She was always the new girl, and she had trouble keeping friends. She went through a period where the Black kids wouldn't play with her because she was the White kid, and the White kids would abandon her when they found out she was Black.

One event that was very traumatic for her happened when she was playing, and some Black girls who were jealous of her hair cut off her pigtails and made fun of her.

She struggled growing up because there was no structure in her life, and she was left alone, so she ventured down a dark path. She's open about how all this affected her mentally. She started drinking and smoking weed at a young age. She, too, suffered from depression; she not only considered suicide, but she also attempted it on several occasions.

After she and her mom moved out of town, she would visit our dad's side of the family, the Sonniers, whenever she returned. This would fill the void she was missing for the short time she was with them. The Sonniers were her connection to our dad. And having that connection gave her peace, though it was short-lived. Whenever one of Earl's siblings passed away, she felt like she was losing our father all over again.

She felt like when one of our uncles or aunts passed, another part of our father was gone. She was losing that connection with him. She said she didn't realize until recently, after our aunt Earlene passed away, that the link to him is me, her brother, not just our dad's siblings. She knows we will always have a link to our father because we are the link.

When Shelly was growing up, the first hint that she had a brother came from our cousin Stasia. Shelly and Stasia had a big argument when they were little kids, and Stasia said, "That's why you have a brother, and you don't know it." She even went as far as getting a picture and showing Shelly this little boy's picture as proof that she had a brother she didn't know about. Shelly ran to her mom and asked her about it. She said, "Mom, do I have a brother?" Mary Jane said, "You may have a brother." Her mom had heard rumors.

Our cousin Stasia's family spanked her when they discovered she had told Shelly she had a brother. She was told from then on to keep quiet about Shelly having a brother. Whenever Shelly asked somebody in the family about it, they would say, "No, you don't have a brother." It was the secret that no one was supposed to talk about. Considering the traumatic things that she went through in her life, she longed to have a brother to share some of those things that she was going through.

As an only child, she would always speak to herself from loneliness. She hated being an only child.

When she was 16, she received a phone call saying she needed to come to Lafayette for a family emergency. My aunts and I surprised her at the airport. Her dream was realized: she was not an only child. She had a real, flesh-and-blood brother, but just as quickly, her emotions began to run the gambit. Her first reaction was shock. Then she felt angry. She was her father's only child. He was gone, and she didn't want to have to share his memory.

Then, she thought back to when she always wanted a brother or sister, and lo and behold, there I was—the brother she always wanted. She began to calm down, and the excitement set in about having a brother. She had always been an only child—and thought she was her dad's only child—and now she had a brother.

After getting to know me and my story, she discovered I had a sister and brother. Shelly said it bothered her having to share me with them. But then, after getting to know me, she felt like I was part of her world, which is what mattered most. Because I wasn't in the first 16 years of her life, she just wanted us to be together all the time. After some time, she learned to love me and knew I was there for her even if I wasn't physically there, and it felt like I was there the entire time.

When Shelly met my sister Mikula and brother Eric, my mom, and Leo, she said she was nervous initially. She wondered if they would accept her and what thoughts they had about her. She said she was always wondering what they were thinking.

When Shelly first met Mikula, she was not happy and got upset. Shelly thought Mikula was bothered because another sister had stepped into the picture. Knowing that Mikula was upset about that bothered Shelly, making Shelly wonder again whether she would be accepted.

Shelly felt insecure, not knowing what they would think about her being a part of the family. But now she had the family she didn't have growing up. She gained another mother, father, and siblings, something she has always longed for. She had a void that started to fill after getting to know her new family.

Shelly loved watching our children grow up. It was meaningful to her that our kids had a chance to grow up together and get to know one another. We had already established our relationship when they came into the picture. Our children didn't know about our family's background story. So, like every other family, they automatically got to know each other, not knowing about the long dramatic story connected to our family.

They were cousins, and they grew up as a family. Shelly said if we had met after we had established our families, it would have been a little different because they would have had to get to know each other while we were doing the same. They didn't have to jump in and figure out how to make this work. Being a family was automatic for our kids.

The Fatal Night

My sister Shelly and I endured a lot in different ways. We lived with a sense of emptiness and self-doubt, for her drugs, and for me, alcohol, to escape what we thought was missing. It led us both to the point of despair, the same place our father found himself, and we found ourselves ready to take our lives just as he had done. It is terrifying to think that my sister and I were close to repeating that unthinkable act with no thought of the people in our lives who might be affected by it.

But the person who was affected the most by my father's death was my Godfather, Albert Green. Everyone calls him Bruh. Bruh was my dad's road dog. He idolized my dad. They did everything together. They were not far apart in age, even though my dad was his uncle. My dad's oldest sister, Teresa, was Bruh's mother.

My father's death hit Bruh extremely hard; he was the last person to see him alive. The thoughts of that day haunted him for years. Bruh turned to drugs and became an alcoholic. His life spun out of control. For ten years, he went through life trying to comprehend what happened, often blaming himself and wondering what he could have done. Bruh was known around Lafayette as someone not to mess with. When he was drinking or doing drugs, he became reckless and dangerous. You would not want to cross him or be on the receiving end if he decided you were the one he would go after. What was worse was that he didn't need a reason.

The demons of that day still grieve him, but he has learned to cope, and with God's help, he has come to grips with that day and the events that transpired. He has been sober for 40 years and has worked very hard to piece his life back together.

It is strange because Bruh and I have never been close. I have vague memories of him as a boy. We spent time together during my freshman year in college when I lived in Lafayette. When I would visit, or someone in the family would pass away, and I attended the funeral, we would spend time together. But it is like there is always a piece of him with me. Bruh is a good man with a giant heart. He loves unconditionally and is fiercely loyal to his family. My father would often tell Bruh to make sure I was alright. The day my father committed suicide, he asked Bruh to take care of my sister if he died.

After I knew the truth about my dad, my uncle Tony ensured that I connected with Bruh. At that time, he talked to Shelly and me about our father. I remember he took us to the gravesite, and it was emotional for all of us. It was my first time seeing my father's grave; for Shelly, it was profoundly moving remembering the dad she had lost, and for Bruh, just painful memories of the times spent with our father.

Because Shelly still lives in Lafayette, she runs into Bruh from time to time. Recently, they had a conversation. He opened up to her about the day our father died. She immediately called me to tell me about their conversation. She encouraged me to call him. A few days later, we were talking, and Shelly reiterated I should call him. When we hung up, I called Bruh. When I heard his voice and his laugh, my heart was filled with joy. We exchanged some pleasantries; we hadn't talked in about fifteen years. I told him about my conversation with Shelly and how she encouraged me to reach out because she felt he was ready to share with us what happened that fatal day. He told me he was glad I called because Shelly read him right. He wanted to share with us because it was part of his healing.

Bruh began to share with me the events of that day.

He was sleeping, and around 10 a.m., my father and another uncle, Clofar, woke him up. They went to the store to buy a few beers. My dad wasn't himself. He drove a few blocks to a house after they left the store. My dad got out of the car and knocked on the door; a gentleman opened the door. They talked for a few minutes, then my father grabbed the man and started to choke him. Clofar and Bruh exited the car and pulled him off the man. They brought him back to the car, but he never told them who the man was and what transpired.

They drove back to my grandmother's house. Bruh drank a couple of beers and fell asleep. My dad woke him up around 4 pm and said they would go out later. Later that evening, they met with some guys they had grown up with and went to a club. Bruh said they were having a good time when my dad called him to the side and said something strange. He told Bruh he didn't want a particular person to attend his funeral. Bruh was shocked that he was talking about his funeral.

He started to cry and repeated the request. When the guys they were out with approached them, my dad asked them to leave. He told Bruh they would leave the club, and they ditched the guys they were with and left. They drove around a while, then stopped at the Peppermint Lounge, a famous club in Lafayette. My dad asked Bruh to wait for him while he went inside the Lounge. Bruh went in, waited about an hour, and then decided to walk home.

As Bruh walked out, my dad drove up, and they left. As they were leaving, Bruh was slightly disappointed because the night was not turning out as he thought. On the drive home, Bruh started thinking about the young lady he was dating and remembered he had heard of a party across town. He started thinking of getting my dad to give him the keys to his car so he could see his girlfriend and go to the party. They eventually returned to my grandmother's house and had a few drinks.

Bruh began to notice my dad's demeanor started to change. He became angry, and, at times, he was crying. He asked my dad to tell him what was wrong, but he only yelled and snapped at Bruh, telling him to leave. Bruh left for a bit but returned to the house. He found my dad crying and unwilling to share what was bothering him. Bruh walked over to a friend's house and asked the friend to call my dad and talk to him, but my dad wouldn't take the call. Bruh returned to the house and pleaded with my father to tell him what was wrong.

My dad told him to leave and get out. When Bruh

would not leave, my dad told Bruh he knew he wanted to see his girlfriend and go to the party. So, My dad gave Bruh the key to his car. Bruh left, but he didn't feel right about leaving my dad alone, so he turned the car around and returned to the house. He went into the house and saw my father sitting on the bed with a shotgun and a paper bag with gun shells. Bruh asked my father what was happening and what he planned to do. They got into an argument. Bruh grabbed the shells, and they argued some more. Bruh could sense the anger and hurt inside my dad. He was able to take the bag away. My father told him to get out. Bruh took the bag of gun shells and handed it to my grandmother, but he was scared to tell her my dad had a shotgun; he told her my dad was not thinking straight and to watch him. As Bruh left the house, my father left the room and said, "You didn't know I had one more." Bruh left the house to head to the party, but it was not entertaining, so after an hour, he returned to the house. Bruh's words to me were, "Your father was dead."

He told me that everything seemed off as he looked back on that day; my father was angry and not acting like himself. He thought for the longest time it was his fault. He said he now realizes that God and his will made this happen. That revelation helped him understand that he can be free from guilt.

He went on to tell me how my father loved my mother and wanted to marry her, but the "colorism got in the way." He said he heard the family discussing forbidding my mom and dad to have a life together because of her skin color. He wanted me to know he loved my mom because she was always kind to him. He reminisced about talking to my great aunt and great great aunt. As we got off the phone, he told me he loved me, and my eyes were filled with tears. I told him I loved him too and that we needed to stay in touch with each other. He said yes, we did.

The Stigma of Mental Health Issues

Many people used to view mental health issues as a stigma. They wouldn't talk about it and, to their detriment, would not seek help with it. Sadly, people ignored the signs. It was easy to dismiss what was transpiring. Thus, people didn't or wouldn't accept and recognize the warning signs.

Because of this, countless people come to abuse alcohol and drugs to compensate for the imbalance in their lives. Unfortunately for my sister and me, this is a reality for our family. As we have gotten older, the stories told begin to paint a picture of a family that struggled with bipolar disorder and depression. This was compounded by heavy drinking and drug usage.

The events that transpired the day our father committed suicide are a classic example of what can happen when someone suffers from a mental illness. The erratic behavior and mood swings, crying one minute, and outbursts of anger the next are signs that someone may be experiencing a mental health crisis. Even him discussing what he wished at his funeral and talking of death were undiagnosed signs of a potential mental health breakdown. Then, I found out that my Godfather suffered from depression for ten years. People believed he was just angry; the fights, the mood swings, and withdrawal from everyone should have been red flags.

Though it is tough to discuss, it is a reality. It needs to be shared because people should be aware that these disorders run in families and understand that they could be passed down to future generations. Shelly and I can attest that we have had our struggles with depression and dependency. This is the case for several of our cousins as well. We have also seen our children suffer with symptoms of mental illness, albeit to a lesser degree.

It is important to recognize signs. The National Institute of Mental Health describes bipolar disorder this way.

Bipolar disorder is a mental illness that can be chronic (persistent or constantly reoccurring) or episodic (occurring occasionally and at irregular intervals). People sometimes refer to bipolar disorder with the older terms "manic-depressive disorder" or "manic depression."

Everyone experiences normal ups and downs, but with bipolar disorder, the range of mood changes can be extreme. *People with the disorder have manic episodes or unusually elevated moods in which the individual might feel very happy, irritable, or "up," with a marked increase in activity level. They might also have depressive episodes, in which they feel sad, indifferent, or hopeless, combined with a very low activity level. Some people have hypomanic episodes, which are like manic episodes but not severe enough to cause marked impairment in social or occupational functioning or require hospitalization.*

Most of the time, bipolar disorder symptoms start during late adolescence or early adulthood. Occasionally, children may experience bipolar disorder symptoms. Although symptoms may come and go, bipolar disorder usually requires lifelong treatment and does not go away on its own. Bipolar disorder can be an important factor in suicide, job loss, ability to function, and family discord. However, proper treatment can lead to better functioning and improved quality of life.

Symptoms of bipolar disorder can vary. An individual with the disorder may have manic episodes, depressive episodes, or "mixed" episodes. A mixed episode has both manic and depressive symptoms. These mood episodes cause symptoms that last a week or two or sometimes longer. During an episode, the symptoms last every day for most of the day. Feelings are intense and happen with changes in behavior, energy levels, or activity levels that are noticeable to others.

Though there is much more awareness of various types of Mental Illness, it is essential to recognize the symptoms and reach out for help. Getting help if you see or suspect someone is struggling is just as vital.

Forgiveness

Forgiveness must go beyond ceasing to blame or holding resentment against someone, which is the more technical definition. You must be willing to understand certain things to forgive someone truly. You must realize you can't control what other people do or say. You are not in control of anything.

Once you know that you have no control over what people do or say, then that's when you can learn to let go completely. What's happening to you is what God is dictating. So, to be free and be able to forgive, you must understand that God is the one who's presenting these things to you. So, learn to forgive. It's easier to start dealing with the negative things in your life once you forgive.

Forgiveness is essential to me because, at one point, I felt a lot of resentment and hatred toward Leo. When my mom and I finally had the conversation about Leo not being my father and how he treated me, I hated her for allowing it to happen.

There was a lot on my hate-hit list. My real family is the Sonnier family. Why would you guys do that to me and my sister? Our extended family would tell us the truth.

But somehow, in the end, it all worked itself out. In the end, we became a family. Now, to make it work, there were many people that I had to open my heart to and say, "Okay, I forgive you". What I was holding in, the resentment towards them, was toxic. Leo and I reconciled a long time ago, and that relationship has done nothing but flourish. Now we talk and enjoy our conversations. He is my father. He is the only dad I have ever known, and though we didn't start great, we are finishing this life strong.

As I said, he is like George Jefferson from the TV show "*The Jeffersons.*" He has a great wit and something to say with a bit of sarcasm. He's not a boisterous man. He calls me now just to tell me a joke, and that's it; we laugh, and then he goes, okay, I know you're busy. Then he will hang up the phone. He loves to call me about something he saw on the news. He will say, I can't believe you all are reporting this. And I'll go, that wasn't us. He goes, you're the media, right? Our relationship is now a blessing. During my 59 years on this earth, I have never seen that man cry. He didn't cry at his mother's funeral or his brother's funeral.

The first time I saw him cry was when I was inducted into the Oklahoma Journalism Hall of Fame. That was a touching and full-circle moment. We've never talked about why he treated me the way he did. He never apologized for the way he treated me. But I don't need it because instead of saying it, he has demonstrated by his actions that he was sorry. And for me, that was more important than words. Accepting his faults and working to improve himself shows what a man and genuine father Leo Labbe is.

I love my mom, and I had to forgive her by letting go of the past. We are very close again. We have a great relationship. She was a strong and determined mother. My mom has a lot of empathy. She was always there for her kids' sporting events, choir recitals, and plays. My mom would come to my football games and wrestling matches.

My mom was everywhere. She was super supportive. She wanted the best for us and was very loving toward us. She cared deeply for her children. She worked a 3 to 11 shift as a nurse. She would get up in the morning and make our breakfast before we left for school.

She always cooked our food, and it was on the stove waiting for us when we got home from school. My mom would leave our home on Fridays, drive an hour and a half to Oklahoma City, and pull double shifts to make extra money. She'd come home on Sunday afternoons but then return to work at the Lawton hospital on Monday.

I remember one time when I was around 11 years old, and I was playing football and running down the field. I looked over toward the sideline, and my mom was screaming and running down the sideline with me. She was super supportive of me and the kids.

Forgiveness is essential in life. I understand now that all roads lead to God. He wants us to see Him and know that He's the one who will see us through the challenging things we go through.

We are always trying to fix something, but we must start with forgiving. We must begin to open our hearts and follow God. We also must learn to forget because if you don't forget, then you haven't forgiven. It is best to let it all go. And again, look at the blessings that have happened since letting it go. My mom and Mary Jane, who married my dad, went their separate ways and never communicated, and somehow, they found themselves together and were close friends.

My step-grandmother, Mable, and I shared a moment when she was 90. I did not want to go to her house. I had not visited her in years, and I still harbored resentment toward her because she had mistreated my cousin and me in the past, but my mom said, "Look, it's your grandmother, and you need to go." I went to her home.

She opened the door and stared at me. I asked if she remembered me, and she said yes and invited me to come in. We had a very open and good conversation. As I left that day, she took me by the arm and told me she was proud of me and sorry for mistreating me.

Because God allowed us to open our hearts and forgive, I celebrated her 100th and 102nd birthdays and was a pallbearer at her funeral.

* * *

Epilogue

Every young boy's dream is to please his father and hear, "I am proud of you, son." I chased that dream in every way possible for 18 years. I worked hard, did well in school, and was the best example to my younger siblings.

I didn't get in trouble. I was a good child. I did it all for my father's approval, but it seemed like the older I got and the more I accomplished, the more my father ignored me. I just wanted to be recognized by him in some small way. But for 18 years, I never got the recognition I desperately wanted.

Then, to suddenly learn at 18 that the man I thought was my father was not my father was devastating. The man I tried to please and be accepted by was not my father. It is hard to put into words how devastating that was to me. Then, to top it off, finding out my biological father was dead by suicide left me empty inside because I thought I would never know the love of a father.

But one day, something extremely extraordinary

happened: God found me. One Sunday morning, when I was 21, I got out of bed, and something said, "Go to church," so I went. About four years later, I met my first wife.

She was attending a bible class at the Institute of Divine Medical Research and asked me to attend. I did attend, but it was strange they preached using the name of Yahweh. I went a few times, but I was intrigued by something they said during the class, specifically, "That God and Jesus are one." I couldn't understand how God, the spirit, was one with his son, who is a man, made of flesh and blood. This was intriguing because it was the bond I had always longed for. In this bible class, I found a clear answer to the question that had intrigued me. This enlightenment happened 24 years ago.

I have remained in bible class; amazingly, my family- my mom, my stepfather Leo, and my sisters- have also become involved in learning more about Yahweh. Throughout the years since I started attending the bible classes, I have come to understand it is not only about us knowing Yahweh but also about him knowing us.

It is about him drawing us to him. This is the basis of a father-and-son relationship. I didn't understand this initially, but Yahweh revealed that he allowed me to experience certain things in my life to bring me to Him, my holy Father. The relationship I longed for with Leo has now materialized because my spiritual relationship with my heavenly Father has been realized.

John 17:21-24 King James

21 That they all may be one; as thou, Father, art in me, and I in thee, that they also may be one in us: that the world may believe that thou hast sent me.

22 And the glory which thou gavest me I have given them; that they may be one, even as we are one:

23 I in them, and thou in me, that they may be made perfect in one; and that the world may know that thou hast sent me, and hast loved them, as thou hast loved me.

24 Father, I will that they also, whom thou hast given me, be with me where I am; that they may behold my glory, which thou hast given me: for thou lovedst me before the foundation of the world.

I have now learned how blessed we are and how amazing the love of the Heavenly Father is toward his son.

The relationship our family has received from Yahweh has allowed us to find forgiveness: Leo and me, me toward my mother, my siblings toward Leo, Shelly and her mom, and Shelly and me toward our dad, Earl, and the Sonnier family. It has allowed us to understand the past, embrace the bad with the good, and know that Yahweh is always in control. Yahweh is always with us wherever we go.

It has allowed us to unite and be one in him—a true family led by the true patriarch.

About the Author

Originally from Louisiana, Blaise Labbe is the News Director for the Sinclair Broadcast Group in San Antonio, Texas.

He oversees news operations in 14 Sinclair markets in 6 states. Throughout his prestigious career, Blaise has held many positions in the media field, including photographer, reporter, special projects producer, news operations manager, assistant news director, and news director. He has received many accolades, including the National Minority Business Development Agency's Cornerstone award, Emmys, a Telly, and two National Awards of Excellence from the National Association of Black Journalists.

He has helped develop stories that have won several Emmys and Regional Edward R. Murrow awards. In addition, news stations under his leadership have won various awards, including the Casey Medal for Meritorious Journalism.

In 2024, Blaise was inducted into the Oklahoma Journalism Hall of Fame. Blaise lives with his wife and four children in San Antonio, Texas.

https://www.goodreads.com/BlaiseLabbe
https://www.facebook.com/BlaiseLabbeAuthor
https://www.instagram.com/BlaiseLabbeAuthor
https://www.youtube.com/@BlaiseLabbeAuthor
https://www.linkedin.com/company/BlaiseLabbeAuthor
https://www.pinterest.com/BlaiseLabbeAuthor
https://www.cedricdfisher.com
https://linktr.ee/BlaiseLabbe